God Is

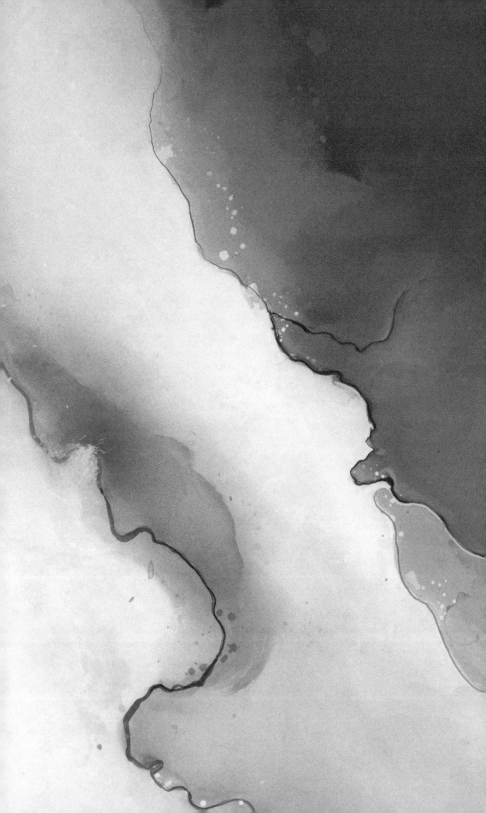

God Is

Mallory Wyckoff

WILLIAM B. EERDMANS PUBLISHING COMPANY
GRAND RAPIDS, MICHIGAN

Wm. B. Eerdmans Publishing Co.
4035 Park East Court SE, Grand Rapids, Michigan 49546
www.eerdmans.com

Published 2022
Printed in the United States of America

28 27 26 25 24 23 22   1 2 3 4 5 6 7

ISBN 978-0-8028-8208-0

Library of Congress Cataloging-in-Publication Data

A catalog record for this book is available from the Library of Congress.

Published in association with Books & Such Literary
www.booksandsuch.com

Unless otherwise noted, quotations of Scripture are from the New Revised
Standard Version.

For Olive and Ivy

Contents

Contents

God Is in the Waves

Expand!
You are not small.
Your foremothers did not do what they did so you could
occupy small!

—Malebo Sephodi

This is, as they call it, my "Jesus year." I am thirty-three years old. I am
a mother of two small girls, living in a city that loves country music
and Southern food. I could do without both (unless Kacey Musgraves
counts, in which case, I like country music). I've never been very
good at math but if we keep things simple and project my lifetime to
be ninety-nine years, I'm one third of the way through. This takes my
breath away a bit. No one, as far as I know, much likes considering
how much closer they are to death than the last time they checked.
But if it's really a Jesus year and I manage to make it past thirty-three,
I suppose I'm doing alright.

I spend much of my time looking back. I'd much rather walk back-
ward and accidentally bump into death than have him in sight the
entire time I make my way down a long hallway. Nobody, I mean
nobody, knows how to handle that situation: *How long are we supposed
to look down at the floor? When is the right moment to look up? Who
acknowledges whom first? (And while we're at it when are we supposed
to use "who" and when is it "whom"?)*

So I look back, and when I do, I see all of the Mallorys that came before: the baby with bleached blonde hair and tan skin, the five-year-old girl with one dimple and baby teeth, the preteen with bangs (oh, God, the bangs), the emo-enough-to-hang-but-I-still-do-my-homework teenager, the high schooler "on fire for God," the responsible college student ready to change the world, the bride who forgot to buy wedding shoes, the idealist twenty-something beginning her career, the bags-under-her-eyes mama with a newborn hangover, and the one sitting here, smelling my sea salt candle and researching my first tattoo—which, incidentally, still feels a lot like the emo-enough-to-hang-but-I-still-do-my-homework Mallory. (If my predictions are correct, the next version of myself will be best friends with Justin Timberlake and Oprah, and I'm really excited to meet that Mallory and summer in the Hamptons with my pals.)

I love all of these Mallorys. I needed all of them. I did not leap my way to thirty-three, managing to avoid bad haircuts and regrettable boyfriends; I expanded my way through each and every phase. Some days I shed skin like a reptile. Some days I tried on a new wardrobe to see how it hugged my frame. And at every turn, I grew more fully into my truest self, including all that came before *and* transcending it. I feel a bit breathless at this altitude, this third-of-life lookout point where I have enough road behind me to make deep reflection worthwhile and miles ahead of me yet to go. But I'm expanding my lungs and inhaling deeply.

This expansion of self has been equal parts painful—the shedding, the releasing, the subtracting—and blissful—the embracing, the accepting, the growing. But I've known no other option. To stop evolving is to die. The fundamental energies of the universe move it forward, as famed twentieth-century paleontologist and Jesuit priest Pierre Teilhard de Chardin reminded us. I have felt that Fundamental Energy moving *me* forward. At this point in life, I know no other way but to ride the waves as they come.

If you've watched NBC's *The Good Place*,[1] you remember the scene of Chidi and Eleanor's final evening together. They've lived their lives on earth, they've lived a million lives in the hereafter, and it's time to move forward. Chidi, typically weighed down by anxiety and brilliance and a crippling inability to make decisions, is uncharacteristically calm. Eleanor doesn't share his peaceful energy, having opted instead to spend the day rehashing highlights with Chidi and dragging him to his favorite places on earth in hopes of keeping him around. She isn't ready to let him go.

She knows what has been and doesn't know what will be, and she wants so much to stay in the now. But there's an energy pulling Chidi forward, one Eleanor did not create and one she cannot stop. And so at last she relents, and they spend their final evening together looking out over a sunset.

Eleanor: "I was never good at being sad, partly because my mom straight up told me not to be . . . but this is sad, man. You got a John Locke quote or a piece of Kantian wisdom you can throw at me?"

Chidi: "Those guys were more focused on rules and regulations. For spiritual stuff, you gotta turn to the East."

Eleanor: "I'll take anything you got. Hit me."

Chidi: "Picture a wave in the ocean. You can see it, measure it—its height, the way the sunlight refracts when it passes through. It's there and you can see it and you know what it is. It's a wave. And then it crashes on the shore, and it's gone. But the water is still there. The wave was just a different way for the water to be, for a little while."

Thirty-three years of waves in, I can see them all. I can picture them out in front of me or behind me or within me, whichever it is. I've shown up in the world in different ways, in different skin, and the continued expansion of myself grounds me deeper still.

A few years back I attended a spiritual formation retreat where we were asked to reflect on the major movements of our lives. Putting pen to paper, I began to recall some of the waves, to give them names, to see my life laid out in chapters. An exercise like this is equal parts embarrassing and nostalgic but also profoundly helpful.

Eventually we were asked to repeat the exercise, but this time we were to track the waves of our evolving image of God. With crayons and markers, I began to sketch all of the varied ways I have understood and imaged and experienced the Divine. Despite my total ineptitude with anything artistic, the picture that unfolded was perfectly clear: the waves of my own movement and growth in the world have mirrored how God has shown up and taken form in my life.

It's like two waves in a rhythmic dance, separate from one another but moving as one. In each season of life, with each iteration of myself, I have seen God reflected in multiple lights. I have encountered various images of the God who is all and none of them.

When I was the bleached-blonde, tanned-skin baby Mallory growing up on the beach, God was Father to me. Somehow I managed to win the dad lottery and have only ever known the very best version of a father—one who, while on a family vacation as my brother and cousins dumped bottles of bubble bath into the tub and suds poured out the bathroom door and into the hallway, chose to keep his video camera focused not on the chaos but on my eight-month-old chubby face, gently whispering to me about how much he loved me. When I heard at church that God was our Father, I felt warm and safe. I knew I could crawl in that God's lap and he would read me books and do all of the voices. I knew I would be protected and fought for and have all of my needs taken care of.

When I connected with a group of friends who were also emo-enough-to-hang-but-still-did-their-homework, I sensed a God who was Friend, pulling me toward relationship and connection. I felt seen by God. Adolescence is an adventure in insincerity, desperately trying on personas until you find the one that gets you accepted into the pack (or at least makes you less of a target). To find real, meaningful connection with a God who seemed interested in spending time with me was no small gift. My connection with this Friend grew, and I grew.

4

Growing up in a Christian home, school, and church, I heard endless talk about "God's plan" for my life well before Drake made it cool or *Degrassi* dominated Canadian airwaves. In small and big decisions alike, I came to know God as Guide, one who helped direct my steps and offered wisdom for how to take them. I knew I wasn't alone in the world, making my own way in the vast cosmos. I had a caring and knowledgeable Guide that I could trust, who had my best interests in mind.

In high school while I was on a short-term mission trip to Guatemala, my privilege came face-to-face with poverty, and I was undone. I read parts of the Bible I never had seen before, parts that seemed to indicate that God was terribly interested in matters of justice and care for the vulnerable and was not entirely thrilled with those who amass wealth and power. I was both compelled and confused. How had I managed to spend sixteen years in a faith system where this kind of theology was not even a blip on the radar screen? Until that point, I functioned believing that my humanness was sinful. That I needed to be something other than human and gather often with other Christians committed to the same pretense. That salvation was a way of ultimately escaping our humanity. (The terms may not have been so crass but really only slightly less.)

With all of this humanity avoidance, there wasn't much energy remaining for matters like caring for creation or dismantling oppression. But in a hurricane refugee village in the central highlands of Guatemala, I met a God who was Social Justice Warrior. Inspired by this God, I began to ask questions of everything, slowly at first, gently even, until eventually I was the obnoxious college student asking to meet with my Intro to Theology professor after every class because 7:45 a.m. is the *perfect* time to discuss the ethics of nonviolence.

My questions led me to seminary, and seminary led me to the God of Deconstructed Presence. I thought it would be a season of building on a twenty-something-year-old foundation, steady and sure. Instead, it was a demolition. My peers and I faced complexities and ambiguities and inconsistencies, and I watched how they responded.

Some could not manage to hold it all, to endure the painful process, and they left. Some remained in the program but dropped out of faith altogether. Others fashioned a sturdy set of blinders and progressed through each course, shoving aside and out of sight everything that threatened their preexisting perspectives.

We all have ways of surviving when we feel threatened, and I am certain some people would rather face a mad gunman than expose their faith to scrutiny. The fear is just too great. I've never been immune to this fear; I know what it feels like in my body. But I also knew that half-assing this journey could never be an option, that during my time in seminary I had to commit to a deep dive into whatever surfaced as I explored faith. The deconstruction was disorienting and painful, but I was not alone in it. Even when I no longer knew what I meant when I said "God," I knew this unknown God was present. Deconstructed Presence held space for me, as together we sat in the darkness waiting long enough for a spark of light to emerge.

There have been more Mallorys and more images of God than can be named here. But suffice it to say that my self-exploration has always led me to a deeper and broader experience of myself *and* of God. I cannot separate these parallel movements any more than I could separate a wave from the ocean.

I've set out to write about the expansiveness of God because there are too many energies that resist this notion, that seek to keep God— and humanity—small. I don't mean God's size. Plenty of people and Sunday school songs will tell you God has "the whole world" in God's hands, that God is all-knowing and all-powerful. But behind these grand notions of God's capabilities tends to lie a small and narrow conception of what God is actually like.

It's as if many believe that one image of God is sufficient, capable of holding all that we are and all that we will be, able to contain all that God is. But my reality has never reflected that. My journey has included this small God. And my journey has moved me forward. A small God—a small *you*—has never served the world.

God Is Hiding under the Table

Stop acting so small. You are the universe in ecstatic motion.

–Rumi

Whoever you are, no matter how lonely,
the world offers itself to your imagination,
calls to you like the wild geese, harsh and exciting—
over and over announcing your place
in the family of things.

—Mary Oliver, "Wild Geese"

The first time I saw pornography, I was five years old. I was playing at a friend's house, a sprawling home full of long hallways to run and ample toys to play with and closets stacked with *Playboy* magazines. The collection belonged to her dad, a gregarious man I only recall as being tall and loud and mostly not around. But even when he wasn't there, the magazines were. Recalling the scene is difficult, because it highlights the absurdities of the situation: two little girls and a bedroom floor covered with dolls, toys, stuffed animals, and porn.

Before I'd lost a single baby tooth, I became aware of my sexuality. I had no concept of or context for understanding what I was seeing. All I knew was the curiosity I felt. Something told me this was wrong, but that didn't stop me from looking. It only made me feel terrible for doing so.

Had this been an isolated moment, its impact may not have been so profound. But there were multiple occasions in my early childhood years—with friends, with neighbors—where this scene repeated itself: innocence, playfulness, curiosity, confusion, shame. I felt the same disturbing mix of emotions and urges and desires and awfulness. It was far too much for my still-rapidly-forming brain and body to know what to do with. I was in kindergarten.

I remember once playing under a table in my classroom, looking at the picture on my lunchbox. It was a Lisa Frank drawing, full of bold colors and magical creatures, but my confused little brain imagined the scene as naked bodies. Instinctively, I knew to hide this secretive play under the table. It was something to keep hidden. *I* was something to keep hidden. Thus began my adventure in staying small.

At the same time, I excelled in the classroom. I absorbed the material and completed tasks quickly, while kids around me struggled to finish. It felt good. Pride surged within me, and I recognized how differently it felt in my body than the shame I carried.

Shame told me I was a bad little girl, dirty for what I had seen and for how I had liked it. Shame told me to hide my play and keep my secrets. But when I excelled in school, when I worked quickly and answered the questions correctly and impressed my teacher, I was able to come out from under the table for a while. I was able to convince myself for a few moments that what shame said about me wasn't true, and even those few moments were the relief I needed.

Shame covers the body and spirit like a weighted vest, and no one—fully grown adult or five-year-old girl—has the capacity to wear it forever. Academics and performance and achievement became my out, my way of managing the shame and projecting a successful image. And it worked. It worked in kindergarten at the table of blocks. It worked when I was captain of multiple sports teams. It worked when I walked across the stage as salutatorian in my high school graduation. It worked when I earned eighteen credit hours in a single month of undergrad. It worked when I was hooded and wore velvet trimmed robes with a newly minted doctorate.

It worked, until it didn't.

Four months after I completed my doctorate, my first daughter was born. Olive was fierce from the womb. In her twenty-week ultrasound picture, she flaunted a head bowed down with a fist in the air. "Oh God, may she use this to resist the patriarchy and not me," I prayed.

I had always wanted to be a mom, but not in the way other women around me wanted. Growing up, their vision boards were full of photos depicting blissful motherhood, being surrounded by children and scheduling playdates and planning craft time and baking chocolate chip cookies.

During spirit week in my senior year of high school—when students dress up in costumes and school colors and for five days feel sweet freedom from uniforms—one of the days was themed "What You Want to Be When You Grow Up." Several of my closest friends stuffed pillows under their shirts and went as pregnant women. I did not. (Incidentally, I went as a medieval pub wench because it was the only costume I could find last minute at Thrift City but honestly I think in twenty years my therapist will help me see what it really meant.)

It's not that I didn't want to be a mom. It's just that in my very long to-do list of things I wanted to accomplish, it was in the "to get to when you have the time" category and somewhere below the "consider another doctoral program" line.

When this always-future-tense experience of motherhood suddenly thrust itself into my present reality, it managed to knock down the entire infrastructure I had expertly been crafting for more than two decades. From my earliest experiences of shame, I had worked relentlessly to keep myself small, hiding who I was, while at the same time striving to achieve and succeed. I set goals and worked hard and performed for others because in this arena, I was good. I could project the safe parts of myself and be something more or something other than a sinful little five-year-old girl.

Chapter 2

When I became a mom, suddenly I was not on a stage or holding a mic or receiving praise. Suddenly, I was spending most every moment home, hidden, utterly exhausted with no time to take a shower, much less promote my curated image to the world. It's hard to really commit to image curation when you're wearing Depends and leaking breast-milk on the sofa and discovering that hemorrhoids are not reserved for the final decade of life.

Each one of my favorite outlets for managing shame was no longer at my disposal, and I was left with the shattered pieces of what had been my identity. It was the hardest thing I've ever experienced. It was the greatest gift I've ever been given.

In that same season of life, I engaged the Ignatian Exercises—an intense, contemplative, months-long series of meditations intended to help open one's eyes to the Divine in their midst. I wasn't sure I had enough energy to contemplate much of anything. But like the good student I am, I sat down one evening and looked at the day's assigned reading. It was Luke 7. Over the years I've shed a lifetime's worth of assumptions about sacred text and how it functions and I've wrestled with every one of the Bible's complexities, but I've never lost a love for glimpsing the Mystery that is God in the pages.

I read the story about a woman who, in the middle of a religious leader's home, anoints Jesus with an expensive bottle of perfume, washing his feet with her tears and drying them with her hair. I watched the scene unfold in my imagination, sensing the woman's grief and sincerity. I observed the religious leaders' shock and disdain. I listened in on Jesus's conversation with Simon about coins and debts. And I asked myself, "Where am I in this story?"

I assumed I'd identify with the weeping woman. After all, I was in a heavy season full of tears—mine as much as my baby's. But I did not find myself there. Degrees in theology framed on the wall behind me, I thought I might identify with the religious leaders. But I did not find myself there. I scanned the scene over and over in my mind until finally, there I was: sitting underneath a table in the corner of the room, away from the action and conversation. I was hidden.

I had often used the word "hidden" to describe my season of early motherhood and the grief I felt in it, the confusing experience of loving your baby and feeling so grateful to be her mom but feeling desperate for the kinds of attention and affirmation I was used to receiving. For years these frenemies had helped me manage my shame and suddenly they were gone and I was hidden: in my house with a newborn, under a table in Luke 7.

I sat there a while, allowing myself to sense the full experience. Then I noticed Jesus, having ended his conversation with Simon, walk slowly over to the table where I was crouched underneath. With love and care, he bent low and joined me there. He didn't say anything, and I didn't either. We just sat, together. Hidden under the table.

That moment didn't heal me, but it set in motion a long journey of making sense of my story and my identity. I began to see how magical this painful season was, a pain that I slowly stopped fighting and finally surrendered to, knowing in my core that it was leading to a better way. I began to reflect on the expert-level tightrope walk I had managed for decades, balancing between succeeding and performing and garnering praise from others on the one hand, and not revealing too much of myself on the other hand. It required surgical precision, ensuring that I was visible enough to prove that shame was wrong about me, and hidden enough to not allow it the chance to tell otherwise.

"Don't do too much. Don't say too much. Don't take up too much space. Don't *be* too much," shame would remind me.

The balancing act was torturous, a complex mix of motivations that churned together inside my body and bound my stomach in knots. I had to perfectly balance visibility and secrecy, exposure and concealment.

Becoming a mom was the first fatal blow to this tightly refined shame-management system. I could no longer balance visibility and hiddenness. I only had the latter. The scales tipped and I was flooded with all the parts of me I had tried to run from. Piece by piece, the system tore away, revealing the scared, confused five-year-old girl managing it.

Chapter 2

My journey with myself and my journey with God have been one and the same. My processes of healing have been guided by expansion, shifting from the tightness and smallness of my finely tuned shame-management system to the bigness, the grandness, the abundance of my true self. It is, in fact, the precise thing that shame warned me of: becoming big, taking up space, being *full*. But I've hopped the fence. I've fled that scarcity. And I know enough of this other way that I can never go back.

My thoughts on God have followed a similar trajectory, one from limitedness to abundance. As a child I was given one or two metaphors for God—all decidedly masculine, and at the time, all helpful. These images worked, until they didn't.

With each season of myself I sensed that there was more to who God is than a metaphor or two could convey. So, I set out to explore the More, and I found it. I found God dwelling in images and expressions and ideas and experiences that I never had been given permission to see as holding such divine possibilities.

Moses didn't know God inhabited bushes until he saw one on fire with the Holy. I think he kept his eyes open a bit wider from then on, granting himself greater permission to see and sense God in surprising ways. I bet, like me, he found himself expanding as his concept of God did the same. I bet, like me, he had his detractors.

As I pursued the More, I began to hear warning bells. I was familiar with internal alarm systems, programmed to project shame's announcement any time I began to be too much or take up too much space. But this time, the warning bells weren't within. The sirens were coming from ministers, from my community, from my tradition. "These explorations are not safe. It's good that you want to know more of God, but don't go thinking God can be found in the places you're seeking." For these folks, my pursuit of the More was unorthodox, agenda-driven, and dangerous. They rang their warning bells loudly.

This sound was not a new one. It simply echoed the warning sounds that have been issued across centuries of church teaching, steeped in certain ways of viewing God and humanity and structuring those ideas and those people in very particular ways. Much can be said about these structures of power and thought, but here's my sense: if we were to pull back the curtain, to see beyond the exterior, I think we would find something like a scared five-year-old managing the systems. We'd find the same fear and shame that dictated my every move and called every shot for decades. I think we'd find that what happens on the micro/individual level has been happening on the macro/systemic level for as long as humans have walked the earth, seeking to make sense of how they got here and what a concept of God could even mean.

There have always been risks to revealing myself, to taking up space, to stepping fully into who I am. But the risks of *not* doing so have always been greater.

There have always been risks to stepping beyond the boundaries that others have drawn around God, to opening ourselves to the More, to naming God with different names. But the risks of *not* doing so have always been greater.

When Jesus joined me under the table that day as I meditated on Luke 7, I knew that whether my smallness in that season was fueled by self-preservation or by my circumstances or a combination of the two, I could not stay there forever. My playing small was no longer serving me, nor was it offering anything to the world. I remained there under the table for a time, hidden, with a God who is gentle enough to join new mamas in their exhaustion, close enough to be glimpsed in the ordinariness of daily life, and More—always More—than I could imagine.

Eventually, it was the abundance of God that drew the five-year-old girl out from under the table in kindergarten. It was the abundance of God that shifted the thirty-something-woman from smallness to fullness. And it is the abundance of God that draws me to write this book, seeking to name the Divine in all the ways I've encountered it.

There is risk here, yes. Maybe you hear your own alarm bells sound off when you consider crossing the boundaries drawn around

God—by you, by your community, by systems thousands of years old. There is risk to any new venture. But this risk also offers wide open space to explore and uncover new ways of thinking about, imaging, and connecting with the Divine.

For me, that space has been wide and rich and fruitful even as countless other aspects of faith have crumbled or come into question or broken away. I long for you to know that kind of expanse, that kind of wide-open space wherein God can be seen and heard and experienced in myriad ways—ways that unsettle and discomfort and disturb, ways that enlighten and inspire, ways that speak grace and peace, ways that lead you to live more fully from your truest self as one who bears the image of this multi-imaged God.

Augustine—one of the most influential Western theologians—stated that if something can be comprehended, then it is not God, since God exists beyond comprehension.[1] This may seem like terrible news for someone seeking to write a book about God, but I agree with him. The God we will speak of here, the God we will seek to name and image and experience in new ways, will still remain Mystery, never able to be fully understood. And this is really *good* news. If the One Who Is beyond Knowing is still somehow able to be glimpsed and perceived and experienced through various images and metaphors, why would we not accept the invitation to do just that—to explore this wide-open terrain?

There is no option for mastery here, no possibility of perfecting something or cracking the code or solving a mystery or having to determine the *one* right answer. There is just an invitation, extended open to you, to explore the God whose essence can be glimpsed in a million ways.

3

God Is More Than We've Been Led to Believe

Tell me what your God look like, Celie.
Aw naw, I say. I'm too shame. Nobody ever ast me this
before, so I'm sort of took by surprise. Besides, when I think
about it, it don't seem quite right. But it all I got. I decide to
stick up for him, just to see what Shug say.
Okay, I say. He big and old and tall and graybearded and
white. He wear white robes and go barefooted.
Blue eyes? she ast.
Sort of bluish-gray. Cool. Big though. White lashes. I say.

–Alice Walker, *The Color Purple*

In a college course I teach that introduces the basic tenets of the Christian faith, I ask students to practice a specific exercise. Before I begin
introducing concepts or offering my sense of what this whole thing
is about, I want to know what these students believe about God.

I don't mean what they say they believe, or how they would answer
that question on paper. I want to know the image that surfaces in their
mind, the feelings they sense in their bodies when they hear "God."
I want to know what associations they make at a subconscious level
to which they give little thought but that are operating in a powerful
way nonetheless.

I ask them to find a comfortable spot, to sit quietly, to close their
eyes, and begin picturing God in their mind. *What does God look like?*

What do they feel? What do they notice? On occasion a student will name something about feeling a sense of warmth in their body or seeing lots of light. But most often, the responses I get boil down to one image: an old bearded man, dressed in a white robe, surrounded by clouds in heaven. It's the same image depicted in art forms as varied as Michelangelo's *Creation of Adam* and the iconic *Far Side* comic series.

If I were to ask these same students whether God was an old, bearded White man, they likely would say, "Of course not. God is spirit. God is not bound to a specific gender or age or race." And they would be right. But it doesn't matter much, does it? It doesn't matter what we say we think or believe about God when, in reality, lying just under the surface of every thought or image or idea we convey about God is this default notion of God as an old male figure in the skies.

This comes up often in my work as a spiritual director.[1] Part of my task, I am convinced, is to help people identify their working image of God. In my sessions I ask lots of questions, and one of the most common is this: "What is the image of God behind that?" When people share what they're thinking or believing to be true, there is always some functioning image of who God is behind that thought or belief. But this image most often remains hidden to us, until perhaps a meddling spiritual director asks us to consider it.

Whatever the thought—that they're not doing enough for God, that they'll never fit in, that God is calling them to a new job, that they need to pray more—there is some particular image of God behind it. Sometimes the image is good and true and full of life; many times, it is not. But it's not until we bring it to the point of articulation that we can even begin to know which it is, and whether we buy it or not. Once we can name the image of God behind our thought, we can more clearly assess whether it's one worth holding.

I'm convinced that what we believe to be true about God informs what we believe to be true about everything and everyone, ourselves included. And this isn't just true for folks who claim the Christian narrative. Christians don't own the concept of God. Every culture and religion the world over has held some notion of the Divine, defined in various and unique ways. Whatever qualities we ascribe to God, however we make sense of God's connection—or lack thereof—with the world and with our embodied realities necessarily shapes our views of everything else. The symbol of God *functions*, as Elizabeth Johnson wrote.[2] The values and identities we believe inherent to God inform our own values, our own identities.

This is why, whether I am teaching college students or sitting with someone in spiritual direction or finding a rare moment of quiet to pray, I so often raise the questions "What is our image of God? What do we see and feel and sense when we picture God?" These questions matter, and they're worth asking.

And yet, what is revealed in the by-and-large unanimous image my students and directees hold of God—i.e., an old White man in heaven—is this: we have an absurdly truncated view of God. Of all the possible metaphors and pictures and ideas and experiences and images of God available to us, much of the church historically has spoken of and thought about and prayed to a God who is, in essence, an old White man. How did we end up, even still in the twenty-first century, with such a narrowed and small view of God? And if it's true that what we believe about God necessarily informs what we believe about everything and everyone, then how has our virtually singular notion of God cut us off from a treasure trove of images and ideas about the world, about our neighbors, and about ourselves? We need to know that we didn't arrive at this place of small, limited thinking by accident.

A few days ago, my daughter Olive and I sat reading a children's book about great trailblazers in history, like Sojourner Truth and Ada Lovelace and Dolores Huerta. With each description of the person's life and work came words like "inequality" and "suffrage" and "slavery" and instantly, I wanted to throw the book down and grab instead the innocent rhyming book about ladybugs that requires nothing of me but to read in rhythm.

Instead, I read aloud words with definitions I did not want to name, definitions about which I was certain she'd ask. Before my girls were born I started gathering a beautiful collection of books for them that empower little girls and encourage their individuality. I've honored their abilities and affirmed their capacity to be and do anything. I work hard to live fully from my own place of empowerment so they can see it modeled. But here it was, a moment I could not hide from. I had to explain why these kinds of books were necessary in the first place.

I had to explain that not everyone values girls and women. I had to share that for many years women weren't allowed to vote or own property. I had to name that Black and Brown women in particular have endured immeasurable oppression. I had to talk about the realities—past and current—of being a girl in the world. I wanted to cry.

Everything in her life up to that moment told her, "You are strong and fierce and brave! You matter! You can accomplish anything!" But in that moment, she came face to face for the first time with the ugliest realities of the world, the ones that she'll bump against and wrestle with her entire life.

I once heard a Jewish professor say that she didn't read the Bible with her small children because it was full of violence and sexism and so on. I totally understand this. There's no shortage of difficult texts in the Bible, and I've wrestled with all of them. But what's worse is that I cannot say to my daughters, "Don't worry, loves. There are some difficult parts of our human history and sacred texts, but people of faith have always understood that all humans bear the image of God, each full of inestimable dignity, value, and worth. The church is a safe place for women and girls and people of color, a safe place for you." I make it a practice not to lie to my girls, but, God, sometimes I wish I could.

So I have to say things like "The truth is that yes, Olive, I did throw away the Frozen lip gloss because it had red dyes in it and I'm the kind of mom who worries about those kinds of things, and yes, Olive, the world and the church have long dealt women a shitty hand."

Children's books about women trailblazers expose some of the skeletons in the closet, but church history puts the horrid reality on full display. From Christianity's earliest days, the greatest theologians and church leaders have spoken of women as the source of all evil in the world, as weak and illogical beings, as temptresses plotting how to lure men into their trap. You may know nothing of church history or its most famed theologians, but I'm willing to bet you know misogyny when you read it. Buckle up, ya'll:

Origen (Greek theologian, second–third centuries CE)
- "Men should not sit and listen to a woman . . . even if she said admirable things, or even saintly things, that is of little consequence, since it came from the mouth of a woman."[3]

Clement of Alexandria (theologian and philosopher, second–third centuries CE)
- Regarding women: "The very consciousness of their own nature must evoke feelings of shame."[4]

Tertullian (Father of Latin Christianity, second–third centuries CE)
- "And do you not know that you are (each) an Eve? The sentence of God on this sex of yours lives in this age: the guilt must of necessity live too. You are the devil's gateway; you are the unsealer of that (forbidden) tree; you are the first deserter of the divine law; you are she who persuaded him whom the devil was not valiant enough to attack. You destroyed so easily God's image, man. On account of your desert—that is, death—even the Son of God had to die."[5]
- "Woman, you are the Devil's doorway. You have led astray one whom the Devil would not dare attack directly. It was your fault that the Son of God had to die, you shall always go in mourning and rags."[6]

John Chrysostom (Archbishop of Constantinople and Doctor of the Church, fourth century CE)
- "Among all the savage beasts none is found to be so harmful as woman."[7]
- On Eve's sin as reason for women to be silent in church: "The woman taught once and ruined all . . . the sex is weak and fickle. . . . Man was first formed, and elsewhere [God] shows their superiority."[8]

- "God maintained the order of each sex by dividing the business of life into two parts, and assigned the more necessary and beneficial aspects to the man and the less important, inferior matter to the woman."[9]

Augustine (Bishop of Hippo, Doctor of the Church, and Latin Father, fourth–fifth centuries CE)

- "I don't see what sort of help woman was created to provide man with, if one excludes procreation. If woman is not given to man for help in bearing children, for what help could she be? To till the earth together? If help were needed for that, man would have been a better help for man. The same goes for comfort in solitude. How much more pleasure is it for life and conversation when two friends live together than when a man and a woman cohabitate?"[10]

- "... woman was given to man, woman who was of small intelligence and who perhaps still lives more in accordance with the promptings of the inferior flesh than by superior reason. Is this why the apostle Paul does not attribute the image of God to her?"[11]

- "... the woman together with her own husband is the image of God, so that that whole substance may be one image; but when she is referred separately to her quality of help-meet, which regards the woman herself alone, then she is not the image of God; but as regards the man alone, he is the image of God as fully and completely as when the woman too is joined with him in one."[12]

- "Watch out that she does not twist and turn you for the worse. What difference does it make whether it is in a wife or in a mother, provided we nonetheless avoid Eve in any woman?"[13]

Saint Albert the Great (patron saint of natural sciences, thirteenth century CE)

- "Woman is a misbegotten man and has a faulty and defective nature in comparison with his. Therefore she is unsure in herself. What she herself cannot get, she seeks to obtain through lying and diabolical deceptions. And so, to put it briefly, one must be on one's guard with every woman, as if she were a poisonous snake and the horned devil."[14]

Thomas Aquinas (Doctor of the Church, thirteenth century CE)

- "As regards the individual nature, woman is defective and misbe-gotten, for the active force in the male seed tends to the production of a perfect likeness in the masculine sex; while the production of woman comes from a defect in the active force or from some material indisposition, or even from some external influence."[15]

Martin Luther (German priest, theologian, and Protestant reformer, sixteenth century CE)

- "For woman seems to be a creature somewhat different from man, in that she has dissimilar members, a varied form and a mind weaker than man. Although Eve was a most excellent and beautiful creature, like unto Adam in reference to the image of God, that is with respect to righteousness, wisdom and salvation, yet she was a woman. For as the sun is more glorious than the moon, though the moon is a most glorious body, so woman, though she was a most beautiful work of God, yet she did not equal the glory of the male creature."[16]

- "The word and works of God is quite clear, that women were made either to be wives or prostitutes."[17]

John Calvin (French theologian, pastor, and Protestant reformer, sixteenth century CE)

- On why Jesus appeared to women first after his resurrection: "I consider this was done by way of reproach, because they [the men] had been so tardy and sluggish to believe. And indeed, they deserve not only to have *women* for their teachers, but even oxen and asses. . . . Yet it pleased the Lord, by means of those weak and contemptible vessels, to give display of his power."[18]

- "On this account, all women are born that they may acknowledge themselves as inferior in consequence to the superiority of the male sex."[19]

- "Now Moses shews that the woman was created afterwards, in or-der that she might be a kind of appendage to the man; and that she was joined to the man on the express condition, that she should be at hand to render obedience to him (Genesis 2:21). Since, therefore, God did not create two chiefs of equal power, but added to the man an inferior aid, the apostle [Paul] justly reminds us of that order of creation in which the eternal and inviolable appointment of God is strikingly displayed."[20]

John Knox (Scottish clergyman and Protestant reformer, sixteenth century CE)

- "Men illuminated only by the light of nature have seen and determined that it is a thing most repugnant to nature, that Women rule and govern over men. Woman in her greatest perfection was made to serve and obey man."[21]
- "Nature I say, paints [women] further to be weak, frail, impatient, feeble and foolish: and experience has declared them to be inconstant, variable, cruel and lacking the spirit of counsel and regiment [or, leadership]."[22]

I wish I could say these were obscure figures, writing horrible things about women from the fringes like an Internet troll in his parents' basement. But the reality is these men remain some of the most lauded and influential thinkers who fundamentally shaped what we know as Christianity—and who fundamentally shaped what we think about women and about God. In a world where men hold the power, where systems are crafted for men, by men, where women are deemed "defective and misbegotten," "weak and fickle," and the "devil's gateway," there is little chance of God being conceived of as anything but male. It is hard to imagine that while in the mornings Saint Augustine railed against women as being "poor helpmates" with "small intelligence" that in the evenings he prayed to Mother God. His imaginative landscape did not allow for it, and thus, by and large, neither has the church's.

I'm thankful for the ways these church fathers sought to take seriously the person and work of Jesus in the world, and certainly their misogyny is not their only defining characteristic. But it's there, and its impact cannot be overstated: the church has inherited and perpetuated an androcentric, patriarchal theology that has harmed *all* of us.

It's robbed us of countless ways to experience God, to consider ourselves as humans, to order our communities in ways where *everyone* has the ability to flourish.

Because here's the truth: what we say and think and believe about God impacts what we say and think and believe about everything and everyone else. When I cannot see myself reflected in God, it is much harder to love myself well. When I cannot see my neighbor reflected in God, it is much harder to love them well.

And isn't this what people are crying out for, that they be seen as human beings with dignity and value? Whether LGBTQ refugees seeking asylum at the US-Mexico border or BIPOC[23] praying with their feet in protests or Asian American women calling out damaging stereotypes or Indigenous elders decrying the kidnapping and forced assimilation of their children, people who have been forced to the margins—of society and of God-language—are refusing to remain invisible, quiet, abused.

If we're serious about advocating for the dignity of all persons and of creation itself, we must be just as serious about freeing our language and images for God from the shackles they've endured and unleashing the true depth, width, and height of the Divine.

The greatest civil rights activists have always reminded us that none of us is free unless we're all free, that my liberation is bound up in that of my neighbor. And I'm just as convinced that my neighbor's liberation is bound up in God's liberation—liberation from the singular, masculine, androcentric framework that serves a select few and into the expansive, wide-open, life-affirming diversity that is God.

We must be willing to take seriously our own experiences, our own stories, our own realities and see how they reflect the nature of God. We must be just as willing to look at our neighbor's experiences, stories, and realities, with eyes wide open to see where God is revealing God's face in them.

In 2018 I listened to Dr. Christine Blasey Ford's testimony to the Senate Judiciary Committee about her alleged sexual assault by then Supreme Court Justice nominee Brett Kavanaugh. That case and all of its associated chaos had the American public on the edge of its seat, watching and waiting. Many recall the day, some twenty years prior, when attorney Anita Hill shared similar testimony against then Supreme Court nominee Clarence Thomas, who ultimately, like Kavanaugh, was confirmed to the bench.

In all of the noise, media attention, and sparring between opposing parties, one thing was clear: we were in the midst of a massive cultural shift, and women were leading it. It was only a year before Blasey Ford's public testimony that women began using the hashtag #MeToo to publicly share their own stories of sexual assault, resulting in millions of posts and tweets across the globe. This movement, started a decade prior by the powerhouse activist Tarana Burke, has become a household name, and it shows no signs of slowing any time soon. Global momentum has been building slowly and steadily for decades as one by one, vestiges of sexism and the kinds of abuses it engenders have been challenged and dismantled in all spheres of society. There remains much work to be done, but the movement forward is undeniable.

In light of this energy around women's continued liberation, women being freed from the chains of sexual harassment and toxic work environments and unequal pay and the overwhelming prevalence of sexual assault, we are living in a time where a corresponding theological effort becomes essential. As we work to further the liberation of women from oppressive and binding structures, we must also work to liberate God—or, more specifically, our concepts of God—from similarly oppressive and binding structures.

The lives of women have always been shaped and impacted by the social and cultural systems around them. Our concepts of God have always been shaped by these same structures. Some are obvious, overt, and easily identifiable. Others are more hidden, insidious, and invisible. But *all* are at work to determine the ways we think about women, how women think about themselves, the ways women have been free—or not—to live their lives, what we believe women are capable of, and the obstacles women face in every sphere of life.

Likewise, the assumptions we have about God, the ways we image and connect with God, and our core beliefs about who God is have been shaped by systems and structures—some good, many not, all limiting.

Women will continue to move forward and harness the present energy to see freedom and liberation for themselves, for their sisters and friends, for girls and women the world over. And if it's true that God is at work in this movement, that God's heart beats for justice, that God has always been a Liberator, might part of our work be to liberate our conceptions of God? To break the shackles that have contained the ways we think about and connect with God—and thus ourselves?

"If God is worshipped as the guiding reality, the source and goal of all, then the truth is tested by the extent to which the idea of God currently available takes account of accessible reality and integrates the complexity of present experience into itself."[24] We need a God who is bigger than the systems erected to control and contain God, more dynamic than a single set of metaphors can contain, more reflective of the untold diversity of humanity.

It's time to pull down the walls that were built around the Divine, whose image has been hiding in plain sight all along—in midwives ushering new life into the world, in creatives making space for others, in mamas nursing their babies to sleep, in hostesses preparing lavish meals at tables where all are welcome.

4

God Is Communicator

God does not offer himself to our finite beings as a thing
all complete and ready to be embraced. For us, he is eternal discovery and eternal growth. The more we think we
understand him, the more he reveals himself as otherwise.
The more we think we hold him, the further he withdraws,
drawing us into the depths of himself.

—Pierre Teilhard de Chardin

I feel it every single semester that I teach courses to undergrads: the
undeniable reality that the second I open my mouth to speak to a
room full of fifty-five students—no matter what I say, no matter how
carefully I craft my words, no matter how precise I attempt to be with
my language—the words I say run through fifty-five unique interpretive channels and come out in fifty-five unique ways. I cringe as I open
up students' journal responses to a lecture, trying to figure out how I
can somehow grade their papers without actually having to read every
single way that I've been misunderstood.

Occasionally a student really hears what I intended to say. Sometimes they get most of the way there. Many times, I wonder if the
student was even in the room during the lecture. How is it possible that I say X and they hear Y? When I'm really tired and grading
papers at midnight, I begin to question whether Brian is actually

right that I did in fact justify violence for political ends. Maybe I just *thought* I had articulated the ethics of nonviolence when in reality, as Brian so astutely observed, I gave an eloquent rationale for the Second Amendment.

This sort of thing can play tricks on your brain, making you question the entirety of your profession, which requires me over and over again to stand before a group of students and risk being misunderstood. If the income potential for an adjunct professor wasn't so great, I might consider throwing in the towel entirely. But you can't earn $5.50 an hour just anywhere.

As humans, we know well this risk. Any time we put ourselves forward, any time we dare to express ourselves, we are assuming the risk of others not understanding us. There is, of course, the additional risk of their not *receiving* or even *liking* us, but if you're anything like me, that feels much easier to manage if at least I can be certain they've understood correctly the thing about me that they're resisting.

Sometimes the misunderstandings are subtle, less about coming away with the wrong information than about just not having all of it. And then there are cases like the iconic song, "Born in the USA."

Bruce Springsteen penned this classic song in 1984, and Americans have been singing it at the tops of their lungs ever since. Sit through any fireworks show in early July and you're certain to hear it playing, its sheer volume topped only by the unbridled patriotism of every man, woman, and child draped in the colors of the American flag.

"Born in the USA." An anthem defending religious-like passion for one's country of origin and all of its associated values. Except, that's not what "The Boss" was writing about.

In the early 1980s, Springsteen played a benefit concert for Vietnam War veterans, men and women whose lives had been turned upside down by combat and violence and death in the name of their country—the country to which they returned home, finding it full of closed doors and devoid of opportunities. Inspired by his experiences with the veterans, Springsteen penned this song, originally titled "Vietnam." He continued to modify the tune until 1984 when it took the form we're familiar with today, serving as the title track of his wildly successful album.

For so many, this song is an anthem of patriotism, best enjoyed with a hotdog and sparklers. But the song isn't about patriotism. It's about a young man going off to war against a dehumanized enemy ("the yellow man") in the name of a country who refused to care for him upon return or make due on its promises. It's a defiant, prophetic tune, one far more biting than most believe.

The average American is not alone in their misunderstanding. In 1984 President Ronald Reagan invoked the song during a campaign speech: "America's future rests in a thousand dreams inside your hearts. It rests in the message of hope in songs of a man so many young Americans admire, New Jersey's own Bruce Springsteen. And helping you make those dreams come true is what this job of mine is all about."[1] Reagan, like most Americans, heard the song playing a hopeful, prideful tune—"Born in the USA!"—while the one who penned it intended to help listeners glimpse the complexities of their birthplace.

More than a decade later, Springsteen referenced how so few seemed to really get his message. During a 1995 concert he told his audience, "I'm sure that everybody here tonight understood it. If not— if there were any misunderstandings out there—my mother thanks you, my father thanks you, and my children thank you, because I've learned that that's where the money is."[2] Apparently, Springsteen and I both rationalize the constant threat of being misunderstood by the enormous earning potential of our careers.

Adjunct professors and famous musicians are not unique in experiencing this risk. Every artist who has ever made himself vulnerable through expression, every CEO who has ever painstakingly designed the perfect presentation for her board, every lover who has ever tried to put their soul into speech knows deep within themselves that risk is inherent to every form of communication. There are no guarantees in any of it.

The nature of human communication is such that precision, perfection, certainty, and infallibility are just not options. Ask any couple sitting across from each other in marriage counseling. After hours and days and weeks and months and years of learning to be better communicators, ones who compassionately listen to their partners and bravely speak their own truth, this couple still knows that there is no perfect option. There is no way to absolutely mitigate against one party misunderstanding the other's intent, and the breakdown in relationship that can quickly occur.

With all of the risks, it's a wonder any of us is still willing to get married, to pen a poem, to teach a class, to write a book, yet our world is chock full of communicative expression of every kind possible. It's either insanity or a miracle.

The part of all this that strikes me most is not that Bruce Springsteen is willing to keep writing songs, or that couples keep their appointments with therapists to learn how to listen to each other. The craziest part of all of this is that every risk inherent to human communication, God takes on. The One who created all things, set the world in motion, holds it in place, and is leading it to healing—this One willingly enters into the complexities and ambiguities and imprecision of human communication. It's either insanity or a miracle.

When Olive was little, I learned quickly that if I had any hope of communicating to her in a meaningful way, I would need to modify my language. I needed ways of expressing ideas and teaching concepts that were accessible to her. When I wanted her to know that the stovetop was dangerous and that she would need to exercise caution, I didn't offer a monologue about the intricacies of electrical currents and ignition systems—mostly because I understand absolutely nothing about these, but also because it would be entirely unhelpful. What my one-year-old needed was to know that when she approached the stove, it was hot and could hurt her.

So I would bend down to her height, wave my hand in a pausing position, and say "hot." She would repeat me, and though she did not yet know what it meant, she soon understood that I was communicating something important to her, and she would begin to approach the stovetop with caution. And then she made connections to her food being hot and needing to blow cool air on it so it didn't burn her mouth. (And then she thought that when I blew air on her booboo to dry it off before covering it with a Band-Aid, it was because it was "hot," which is a much cuter misunderstanding than Brian's take on my ethics lecture.)

The simple act of inhabiting her language and developmental capacity was one of love. It took time and intentionality and care and didn't always go well, but these are minuscule asks weighed against the overwhelming love for a child.

My sense is that it is love, too, that compels God to inhabit our language. Why else would God take on the risks? Why would God be willing to endure endless sermons claiming certainty about God's will that in fact reflect nothing of God's self or desires or intent? How is it that God has endured millennia of humans making ultimate claims about God and truth that so often look and sound nothing like God when some days I feel like I'll *die* if I hear one more bad sermon? Love.

There is risk in human communication. No options exist to perfect it or guarantee its results or completely safeguard it. It will always be imprecise and complex and messy. But for love, God enters into this mess and dares to speak, dares to be heard, dares to communicate to humanity. Insanity or miracle.

What confounds me more than God's willingness to inhabit human language is that, so often, our response is to clamp down with a perceived sense of certainty and rightness on what we think God says and means, to make absolute claims about divinity and truth, and to then retreat to our bunkers with weapons at the ready to shoot down anyone whose voice or perspective speaks a different word.

We are terrified of the idea that the words of Scripture might hold a plethora of meanings, that they could be a wide-open field in which to run and explore rather than a codified instruction manual. So we carefully craft doctrinal statements about the authority of the Bible and its presumed infallibility and perfection, and we make these demands of sacred texts that, ironically, tell of a God who seems to hold none of the fears we do about communication.

I've heard plenty of preachers and commentators boast that their expressions of God and truth are simply what the Bible says. "I don't interpret the Bible; I just read it," they say. This is, of course, absurd. The Bible did not fall out of the sky penned in modern English. Communities of readers and scholars over centuries have engaged in interpretive acts each and every time they move from the original language of a text (Hebrew, Aramaic, or Greek) to another language.

Decisions have to be weighed at every move and determinations made about how to capture the essence of a text as it's translated into a new language. Some point to this and shout "See! We can't really know anything because it's all just someone's interpretation." But I'm convinced that both camps—the "I don't interpret the Bible; I just read it" folks and the "lost in translation" folks—approach the text in a similar way, that is, with the assumption that interpretation and finitude and imprecision are regrettable aspects of the human reality.

Plenty of theologians have claimed that the need for language and communication is the result of "the fall," the world having been corrupted and impaired. And I don't believe them for a second. I know the risks of human communication, the space between what I intend to convey and the words I use, and the even bigger space between the words I use and how they're heard, received, and understood. This is a risky enterprise, yes, but not bad. Not evil. Not corrupt. Just human.

These vulnerabilities are inherent to the human experience as we know it. We cannot escape them, nor can we overcome them. Either effort devalues creation as it is, which is inherently good. And God as Communicator enters fully into this good creation and inhabits all of its complexities, all of its imprecision, and takes on our forms of communication that we might encounter the Divine.

Barbara Brown Taylor tells a story—and when BBT tells a story, I listen—about the people of Solentiname, a string of islands on the southern tip of Lake Nicaragua. In the 1980s, the Catholic Foreign Missionary Society of America created a biblical commentary series called *The Gospel of Solentiname*. It gathered the voices and perspectives of the islands' people who would sit each week with Ernesto Cardenal—a Catholic priest—and discuss a biblical text.

Instead of offering a sermon, Cardenal sat with hundreds (and at times thousands) of poor farmers and fishers—men and women who were well acquainted with poverty and systemic injustice—to listen. They had endured years of increasing inequities at the hands of Nicaragua's ruling family, and they lived on the edges of vulnerability.

Their discussions included reflections on the well-known parable of the talents, found in Matthew 25:14–30. Read in a different setting, like the one I grew up in, the story has a familiar ring to it. A master goes on a long journey and entrusts money to three slaves—the first receiving five talents, the second two talents, and the third just one (a talent was an enormous sum of money, equal to roughly twenty years of a laborer's wages). The first slave took the money and doubled it. The second slave did the same. But the third slave buried the money in the ground.

Upon the master's return, the first two slaves were eager to share the reports of their successful trading and investments, and the master was eager to reward them. "Well done, good and trustworthy slave" he says. "Enter into the joy of your master!" The third slave, however, didn't receive the same warm response. "Master," he said, "I knew that you were a harsh man, reaping where you did not sow, and gathering where you did not scatter seed; so I . . . hid your talent in the ground." The master, enraged at the slave's ineptitude, condemns him to the darkness "where there will be weeping and gnashing of teeth."

I've heard this text a thousand times and the moral of the story is always clear: God wants people to use their resources, their literal talents, and invest them in ways that prosper God's kingdom. God doesn't want lazy good-for-nothings who bury what they have. God wants scrappy investors with the energy of a stock trader, making smart exchanges and reaping plentiful fruit. Case closed. Amen.

Except, for the people of Solentiname, the conversation went in a different direction. They recognized the master for the wealthy powerbroker he was, "one more tycoon sitting on a pile of money so high that he cannot see the bottom of it, which is why he has to hire people to keep it flowing up from wherever it comes from without troubling him with too many details."[3]

For them, the master in the story could *never* be the God character, and the hero of the tale is neither of the two industrious slaves but rather the third one—the one who buries the talent "where it can't do any more harm."[4] The one who speaks truth to power and calls injustice by its right name. The one who refuses to play in the corrupt game. He is sent where whistleblowers and activists and journalists often end up, forced into the darkness, the shadows, even death. But he goes there a hero.

I'm not interested in speculating who gets the parable "right" because I don't think that category exists (though I'm convinced the people of Solentiname were on to something). I simply want to highlight the reality that so much of what we think and feel and believe is shaped by our social location, by who and what we see—and perhaps even more so by who and what we don't.

We cannot escape this. We can and should acknowledge our limits and try on wider lenses, particularly for the sake of our neighbors suffering just out of focus. We can and should be suspect of our assumptions and expose them to new insights. But we will remain limited, finite creatures who can never truly see the whole picture, who misunderstand texts, who struggle to say what we mean and struggle even more to understand someone else.

This is a messy enterprise, yet right here in the middle of it is a God who speaks in parables. A God who takes on the language of a people. A God who names extraordinary truth in stories about money and fish and fields and widows and wayward children. We'd prefer to think of God in a white lab coat and goggles delicately placing words into thin beakers, isolating them from contamination. But I imagine God sitting in the circle of farmers and fishers in southern Nicaragua, dirt under their nails and sweat on their temples.

I imagine God's delight at the exchange of thoughts and ideas, hearing stories of pain and difficulty woven with celebrations and joys. I imagine God inhabiting the space these interpreters create because it's there that truth and beauty are fleshed out in the messy reality of human existence, when "people of faith get together and let the sharp edges of our real lives poke at that Scripture until it yields new and living truth by the power of the Holy Spirit, maybe even something that would upset the master."[5]

A Jewish scholar once shared with me that Jews tend to think of their sacred texts as a diamond, held up to light. As rabbis share their thoughts and readings, another rabbi will shout, "Give me another one! Give me another reading!" Because they know that engaging God and reading texts and encountering the Divine are not pursuits of a singular end, that the nature of God cannot be isolated and located with a pin on a map. Scripture, she told me, is like a faceted gem, and every time you twist it, the light catches it in a new way and suddenly, you see everything differently.

So, if God is comfortable clothing God's self in symbols and metaphors, in parables and poems, in texts with myriad meanings, maybe we too can embrace the multivalent chorus of images that reflect the Divine and help us catch the gem in a particular light, and then another. There's no chance for perfection here, but my God, there is the chance for beauty.

God Is and Is Not

Words, symbols, and images that do not adequately orient human beings toward life do not adequately name "God" as God.

—Karen Baker Fletcher, *Dancing With God*

If God is male, then the male is God.

—Mary Daly

Before we venture into this risky and imperfect and thrilling terrain of expanding the ways we image and engage God, I want to name a few of the guideposts for our journey. This exploration may feel a bit like dancing to a song you've never heard, uncertain of whether it suits your style and unsure of how to move your feet. So let's begin exactly there: a story about dancing.

Every year, a town just outside of Nashville is host to a summer music festival called Bonnaroo. People camp in the heat and humidity for days, wearing flower crowns and hemp shirts and sometimes nothing at all (things get weird by day four), and spend hour after hour watching musicians of every style perform.

I sweat way too much to camp in the middle of June and I'm not brave (*is that the word?*) enough to forgo showers for access to twenty-four-hour folk music. But sometimes I take my poser self and blend in with the true festival goers to catch a favorite singer or band (turns out I will always be the emo-enough-to-hang-but-I-still-do-my-homework Mallory).

For four days every year, Bonnaroo turns its tiny host town into the seventh largest city in Tennessee, where the people assemble themselves to sing and dance and celebrate life. I love the music and the cultural experience, but what I love most is the silent disco. At first glance it looks like a cult engaging in transcendental prayer or sweaty accountants-by-day having a drug-induced out-of-body experience (which may be true). But then you realize that everyone is wearing headphones, and a DJ is playing music that can only be heard through them, and hundreds of people are dancing to the same song in wildly different ways.

Whether it's a romantic slow jam or Missy Elliott's "Get Your Freak On,"[1] I dance like Elaine from *Seinfeld* because my body offers me no other option. But there's no time for assessing my moves or judging my neighbor's because we're all just in the very weird and wonderful moment. We're listening to the same song but we're expressing it with our bodies in a hundred ways, all in a space that remains totally quiet.

In college I spent a semester studying in Cambridge. One evening, when I probably should have been paying more attention to my Brit Lit course and which King George we were talking about now, I had an idea. What if we could have a silent disco, but everyone listened to *different* songs? What if we weren't restricted to the DJ's singular choice, but we could be our own DJs?

We were a hodgepodge mix of students, some who already knew each other well and some who were starting to date each other and some who had just broken up and some who were traveling outside of the country for the first time and some who had never danced in public and some who weren't sure this was the kind of thing they imagined happening during their rigorous semester abroad in Cambridge. But we gathered a group willing to give it a go. Everyone grabbed their iPods and headphones and queued up their playlists. And a room full of strange, smart, homesick, quirky, idealist undergrads created a silent disco in the back house of a B&B.

It was magic. People danced by themselves. People danced with each other. People played the music they liked, and people grabbed a friend's earbud to try out what they were playing. Greg raged to heavy rock and head banged in the corner. Jesse moved to the addictive beat of Kanye's "Stronger." Hope listened to Arcade Fire sing about the dullness of modernity. Jonathan vibed with an obscure underground indie band that wouldn't be discovered for another year. I closed my eyes and surrendered to the trance that is Sigur Ros. And we all danced.

Every once in a while, I would pause my music and take in the strange and delightful scene: a room, completely silent, full of people dancing freely and enjoying the hell out of the moment. I don't remember a single William Blake poem we studied, but I remember every bit of that night.

If you ever get the chance to attend the silent disco at Bonnaroo, do it. But what I recommend even more is creating your own. A room full of a hundred people dancing to the same song is great, but a room full of people dancing together to a hundred different songs? That is magic.

I share this strange experience as a metaphor for what we're up to here in this book, and as an example of how metaphors work—and, just as importantly, how they don't work. Every metaphor is imperfect and eventually it breaks down. By even explaining my use of the metaphor, I run the risk of breaking it down myself before it even has the chance to function. But hopefully it will work for us long enough, and if not, you've at least now got a fantastic suggestion for your next dinner party.

In the next few chapters, we'll engage symbols and similes and metaphors as ways of getting at what we mean when we say "God." We often talk *about* God, but we don't often talk about *how* we talk about God. For a symbol with as much enduring weight and importance as "God"—even in the midst of an increasingly secularized world—we simply cannot afford to be unreflective here.

"God" functions as a symbol for people's sense of ultimate good and meaning and purpose, the highest order of truth and beauty—and thus, their own internal and external ordering of things. There is a direct correlation between what people think about God and what they think about the world. And if we're seeking a more beautiful world, one wherein everyone and everything is able to flourish in fullness, then we must seek more beautiful and full ways of speaking about God.

So I start down that path by engaging a distinctly feminine set of images and metaphors, for several reasons—firstly, because they've saved my life. I desperately need to know that I am made in the image of God—fully and wholly as I am. When God is conveyed solely in masculine language and within masculine frameworks, I am forced to do a whole bunch of translation so that my lived experience can somehow at best maybe get *close* to God language. In general, this is not something men have to do.[2] They get to be like God in a way I'm not. They simply don't have to engage in this exhaustive translation work because they already hear and see themselves and their embodied reality in words about God—He, Him, Father, King, etc. Feminine language for God allows me to shift my energies away from overcoming the chasm between my reality and God language, and instead to actually *engage* the God Who Is beyond Gender and still somehow able to reveal herself in my gendered experience.

Secondly, I explore feminine metaphors because church history has been so grossly devoid of them that if we were to spend the next two thousand years speaking only of God as She, we just might be able to put a small dent in the image that queues up in folks' minds when they pray.

I've witnessed countless times the difference that it makes in the lives of women—and men—to be given a broader set of language and images whereby they can imagine God. It's a paradigm shift, a total reorientation of the way they understand God and themselves. It's a permission being granted to them that always was theirs but they never knew was possible or even appropriate.

Everyone dancing to the same song can be fun, and that song can hold incredible meaning for many. But why rob ourselves of the chance to hear music as diverse as the universe itself? With infinite ways of expressing truth and beauty and soul through music, why would we ever keep our ears closed to all songs but one?

Sometimes, exploring a feminine image for God can help people hear the song within themselves, realizing that even as they've lived in a world where all other music was silenced, a different tune has been playing within them all along.

Thirdly, I talk about God in the feminine because of what women do when they're allowed access to abundance. It's widely accepted among experts in humanitarian and relief work that one of the best ways to change the world is to empower women and girls. When governments and nongovernmental organizations invest in women, they are in fact investing in entire communities. Women take what they are given—a microloan, access to education, basic healthcare—and multiply those bread loaves and fish to feed their families, their neighbors, their world. The return on investment is maximized to its fullest extent, for the women's own sake and for the sake of their neighbors.

Humanitarian experts also know that far too often, the world does not suffer from a scarcity of resources but rather from the inequitable and unjust distribution of those resources. I long for women to know the Divine in all of her abundance so that, like a small microloan to start a sewing business or policies ensuring access to girls' education, women can embrace this abundance and invite everyone else to share in it. It is here we will see that in fact, this is for *everyone*. It may begin in the particular of feminine language, but like the universe itself it is inherently expansive.

A bigger perception of God, no longer bound by patriarchal norms, is good news for everyone—men very much included. When we're able to see God in fuller ways, we can access ourselves in fuller ways. We can resist the limiting structures and narratives that demand allegiance—even those that appear to be to one's personal profit—and embrace a far richer and more robust world that reflects an equally robust God.

Fourthly, I write about God in the feminine for my daughters. Research shows that children begin to intuit and internalize theological awareness by age two-and-a-half. Like commercial jingles that stick like glue to the insides of your brain whether you use the product or not, the masculine God language my girls will encounter in a million different ways—in religious settings, in art, in culture, in politics— will leave a real imprint. Some of these masculine God images will be lovely and helpful. When they hear God described as Father, they undoubtedly will conjure up the sweetest of images—their dad's patience in teaching them how to hammer a nail, his playful energy that seems to have no limits, the ways he climbs into bed with them each night to read books, slowly and with voices. I *love* that this will be their experience, as it was mine. But it will always be insufficient.

I want for them to have more than a God with whom they cannot identify, a God who does not reflect their embodied reality. I need them to know that as girls and women in the world, they have the very same capacity to reflect God. That when they get their hands dirty in the mud or gently care for one another or paint rainbows on craft paper or assert their voice and agency, they too are helping the world see what God is like.

And lastly, I do it for you. I want to provide a space where you can breathe deeply and feel safe and seen and known, where you don't have to engage in mental and theological gymnastics simply to engage the God whose image you're told you bear but from what you see and hear you'd never know it. If you're a translator-on-the-fly like me, you know exactly what I mean. You hear beloved hymns or participate in liturgy, and you direct your focus to translating pronouns for God and humans just to carve out a small space for yourself in the experience. You expend precious energy on the work of translation—which is essential for your dignity lest you be marginalized by exclusive language one more time—when all you really want to do is reflect on the notion of a God who is Relationship Itself as you sing the Doxology, a God in deep solidarity not with "mankind" but with *humanity*.

Dr. Christena Cleveland, a social psychologist and public theologian, describes what it's like to live as a Black woman in a world ruled by "whitemalegod":

As I've worked through my experiences of trauma I've come to realize that women and people of color are often induced to exhaustively and defensively "play God" because societal institutions (and their whitemalegod) are never looking out for our well-being. If whitemalegod is in charge, then I'm inherently unsafe and I need to try to exert control over anyone and everyone, including myself. So, of course, under whitemalegod's reign, I can never take a moment to rest and just breathe! But the metaphor of the Divine that She Who Restores Our Soul offers us releases us from this grip. If God is a Black Woman, then I don't need to be god. I don't have to be a superhuman who always has to be on guard against myself and others. I can be a regular human and trust that She Who Restores Our Soul has my back.[3]

May this book be a tool for you, for me, for all of us to experience that kind of rest and restoration.

But as with any journey worth taking, there are risks to this one. As I critique a singular notion of God as masculine by offering a sample of distinctly feminine metaphors, I run the risk of remaining lodged squarely in a false binary. My point is not to exchange one set of language for another, to replace "He" with "She" and call it a day. Nor is my point to say that what is deemed masculine is associated only with men and what is considered feminine pertains only to women.

What I'm seeking to do is help expand the ways folks think about God so that they might discover the abundance that always has been there—the jewel waiting to be turned over and over so that light can reveal new and precious qualities. I start with the feminine because it's reflective of my embodied experience as a human being, and this is the only place we *can* start.

You can dress up God language and concepts in fancy, highbrow theology, but the abstract is not where humans live. We live in the flesh and blood, dirt and mud, day in and day out reality of life. If God language cannot find us where we change diapers and care for our aging parents and tend to seeds in a field, then it's not worth the shit we get on our hands when we do so. Good theology is reflective of real life, the life that it then informs and gives meaning to.

My own social location is necessarily limiting, as is everyone's. I am a White, middle-class, straight, cisgendered, able-bodied woman living in the United States. This gives me access to some vantage points, and the likelihood of missing others. My use of feminine God language is neither meant to be exhaustive nor to replace one restrictive binary for another, but rather to say, "There's More here. Will you come explore it with me?"

Another risk we run in this exploration is that every metaphor is imperfect and imprecise and can never grasp truth or reality in their wholeness. We'll talk about God as Mother because I've experienced God as Mother, and because God herself claims the same (Isa. 66:13). But every metaphor—even the most beautiful—is both like and *not like* that which it symbolizes. We are in the realm of human language here, which—as we've named previously—does not allow for totality or perfection or infallibility (though Mary Oliver's poems might yet convince me otherwise). We have no other option but to reach for images and language and symbols to explain the ineffable that is the Divine. So, yes, God is something like a Mother, but also not. God is She, and not She. And so on.

For many people, women especially, trauma is what catalyzes their pursuit of a feminine God. When "father" conjures images of the very person tasked with protecting you but who instead violated your body or diminished your spirit, it's no big leap to reject masculine God language. While exposure to a fuller picture of the Divine can often be healing and sometimes *essential* in retaining any faith sensibilities, I am under no delusions that a language swap will be perfect either. I'll speak of God as Midwife because to me a midwife reflects the best of humans. But there are midwives who harm their patients through carelessness and neglect. I'll speak of God as Home, but for some home is the last space they could associate with the Divine. This highlights my insistence that any singular notion of

God—masculine *or* feminine—is insufficient. I want to add to the collection of God metaphors so that none of us will ever believe we only have one lens through which to view the infinite God who can be glimpsed but never fully.

When I've employed feminine language for God in religious settings, or when I've mined my embodied reality as a woman for deeper understanding of the Divine, I've seen the way it can hold wide-open space for others to breathe and explore and know God. I've also seen the way it pisses people off. Once at a church when I referenced breastfeeding as a means of understanding the sacrament of Eucharist, a man—horrified by what he heard—complained to a friend of mine.

"It's just too much," he said. "Maybe there's room to talk about this kind of stuff in the women's group, but not here. Not with everyone."

His indignation was reflective of far more than his discomfort at hearing the word "nipples" uttered in a sanctuary. It pointed to the ways that we've made idols of language. The world's norms are by and large patriarchal and androcentric, so masculine language, concepts, and frameworks are considered the default. They have the privilege of remaining unquestioned, of appearing neutral.

Within this paradigm, to speak of God as Father is simply to talk about God, but to speak of God as Mother is to have an agenda (or so they tell me). It is to name something "other" than what masculine language would, which is itself distinct and particular but, because of its dominance, gets to parade as being neutral. The distance between the symbol and what it seeks to convey is collapsed entirely, thus becoming literalized and concretized to the exclusion of all else. As Elizabeth Johnson names: "Then the comprehensible image, rather than disclosing mystery, is mistaken for the reality. Divine mystery is cramped into a fixed, petrified image."[4] This is, plainly and simply, idolatry.

Even a cursory glance at the texts Jews and Christians hold sacred reveals God's warnings about idolatry (Lev. 26:1). God has always insisted that the Divine can never be contained in the image of any one created thing, including human language. Our words—about God, and about everything—can only ever be guideposts, but "most people have made them into hitching posts."[5]

So let's move forward in our journey of the Divine looking for every good and beautiful guidepost we can find. When we find them, let's pause and rest at each for a moment. Let's breathe deeply and enjoy every nourishment we might need. Let's linger in the truth and beauty each guidepost can point us to, never confusing the post itself with the vast, wide-open, mysterious, life-giving terrain it helps us explore.

6

God Is Creator

In the beginning, God.

—Genesis 1:1 (NIV)

If the concept of God has any validity or any use, it can only be to make us larger, freer, and more loving. If God cannot do this, then it is time we got rid of Him.

—James Baldwin, *The Fire Next Time*

"Thick thighs save lives." I'm never really certain what this phrase means, exactly, but I do know it's true. When I was fourteen my mother was in a plane crash that by every account should have killed her. In part, what helped save her life were her thick, strong thighs. That woman has been rollerblading all over St. Petersburg, Florida, since the early 1990s, well before twenty-somethings with fanny packs made it ironically cool again. At the gym when men use the leg press machine after her, they sheepishly have to lower the weights. She is *strong*. Minutes before the fourteen-hour emergency surgery where doctors anticipated having to amputate her legs to keep her alive, she overheard the surgeon's comments. "She's built like a brick shithouse!" he said. Thick thighs helped save her life.

I inherited these life-saving thighs, though mostly up to now they've just made it impossible to find good jeans. I have my grandfather's calf muscles—just what every girl hopes for—thick and round. Like him, I sweat like it's as essential as breath, like the moisture on my upper lip and underarms is forming a reservoir in case of a coming drought.

Somehow, I keep managing to make friends with the kind of people who once read something about sweat on the Internet but have yet to encounter it in real life. My best friend—also not a sweat-er— has to hold weights on a stair climber in order to force the steps downward. We've been best friends since we were three and have shared clothes approximately zero times.

I've spent my life navigating these tensions in a world that values women's smallness. All sorts of systems have conspired together to create a supposed ideal, a standard by which bodies in general and women's bodies in particular are evaluated. Even women who work hard to resist these systems and live freely in their frame—whatever it may look like—will tell you that it's hard to exhale self-love when the air around you is laced with stories and images and standards that promote self-loathing.

There are seasons when I wrestle with that self-loathing, when the external pressures to stay small in body collide with the internal pressures to stay small in spirit. But I always come back to my origin story, to the family that made me and whose genes are mine. I realize that even if I wanted to, I can't for a second make these thighs any smaller. They are going to take up their space whether I like it or not. I think, somehow, thick thighs have saved my life.

Our origin stories shape so much of who we are, so much of *how* we are in the world. Making sense of them is equal parts terrifying and liberating. But in the tender moments, perhaps after a few glasses of wine or while sitting with a good therapist, when we're willing to look at our stories with eyes wide open to see whatever there is to see, we discover so much.

I've heard the Bible's origin stories since I was little, since before

I knew to question why anyone would base a child's room décor on a terrifying story about the whole world—save a handful of people and animals—being swallowed alive by water. There are many curious things about the book of Genesis. Perhaps even more curious are the ways its first two chapters have been debated and weaponized and caused some to lose their faith and others to defend it with fury and creation museums.

I'm not all that interested in arguing about how this whole thing came to be, partly because to the best of my memory I wasn't there to see it, and partly because it feels like a lot of wasted energy on the wrong set of questions. It's not to say that the origins of the universe don't matter, or that our stories and theories about the world's inception don't have implications for how we view all who inhabit it. It is simply to say that these stories in Genesis seem much less interested in offering a scientific rendering of the cosmos than they are interested in telling us something about the nature of the Divine—and thus ourselves.

"In the beginning when God created the heavens and the earth, the earth was a formless void and darkness covered the face of the deep, while a wind from God swept over the face of the waters" (Gen. 1:1–2). Before Creator begins making pronouncements—"Let there be light! Let there be animals! And let there be adorable videos of unlikely animal friendships!"—she hovers over a muddy lump of clay like a potter at the wheel. There is this stuff of creation, a "formless void," that she tends to. Before the form is given life and shape, before light dances in the sky and fish splash in the sea, Creator is connected to the formless void intimately, incubating it like a mother hen with her eggs. We don't know how long this went on; this is where the story as we know it begins. But when the time seems right to Creator, she takes the muddy lump of clay and invites it to become something, to take form and shape, to expand.

True to its name (the word "genesis" means "birth"), this is a birth story. And just like a woman who's giving birth co-labors with her own body and with the baby she's bringing forward, the formless stuff of creation labors with God. "The deep, the darkness, the waters dance in co-creative activity with the Spirit of God. Out of mutual, loving creative activity, all that we call life came into [the process of creative becoming]."[1]

Any potter worth her salt will tell you that clay has its own life force, with its own mind and intention for what it will become. Potters sit at the wheel with a result in mind, and with skill they usually can execute it. But they know that the soft mound of dirt resting on the wheel wants to become something. They may even ask the clay and listen for its response, its movement, as they center it on the wheel and feel its grit between their fingers.

Whatever the intentions—those of the potter and those of the clay—whatever the final form, this creative process takes place between the thighs of the artist. When I started studying pottery, the first lesson I learned was to scoot my stool as close as possible and grip that wheel with my thighs. "Don't think you can stay outside of this process," my teacher said. "Get close to it."

I was born between my mother's thighs and my girls came from mine. And there simply is no way to bring about new life without expansion. A mother's body grows, expands, gets bigger. The extent can vary, of course, depending on myriad factors, but the expansion is inevitable.

I was six months pregnant with my second daughter when Beyoncé's *Homecoming* documentary debuted on Netflix. My husband was so enraptured by the awe-inducing performance that he didn't notice I was quietly sobbing beside him. I listened to this queen describe her own body's expansion during her pregnancy with twins, watched her nurse these beautiful babies in between choreography sessions. Equal parts hormonal and amazed, I cried at the sheer beauty of a mama's body expanding to make space for new life. Her body opens up and becomes bigger so that another life can emerge.

This origin story in Genesis is about a God whose own self expands in some way to make room for creation. It is a story of love and beauty, purpose and intent. And it stands out in the collection of ancient Near Eastern creation myths. "Myth" does not simply mean "fanciful story" or "something to be debunked by two nerdy White guys on TV." Myth is a genre of literature through which communities seek to make sense of the world, make sense of themselves and their longings, their conflicts, their fears, make sense of life and its meaning or lack thereof. As long as humans have walked the earth, we've looked around at the cosmos—to whatever extent we see and understand it—and asked, "How did we get here? What is this all about? Who are we in the midst of an infinite universe? And where is this whole thing going?"

From as early as 1700 BCE, we have record of how some ancient communities have sought to answer these questions. In some ways, their accounts bear remarkable resemblance to ancient Israel's, and in other ways, they are markedly different. Conflict and violence are central features, where gods battle one another to earn the top spot in the pantheon.

In one story,[2] the god Apsu and goddess Tiamat emerge as supreme from a host of smaller, louder deities. Their noisiness bothers Apsu, like an old man infuriated at a child's audacity to step on his grass, so he plans to murder them (I'm sure the old man with the lawn has at least *considered* that possibility). Catching wind of the plot, the little gods preempt the strike and take down Apsu. Enraged, Tiamat seeks revenge by attempting to murder their leader, but ultimately she loses the battle. Her carcass is divided into pieces to become the sky, and her eyes—buried under a mountain—become the sources of the Tigris and Euphrates rivers.

Another account[3] tells of a caste system of gods, the lower caste being forced to engage in taxing labor. Growing tired of their work, they plan to battle the upper caste of deities to overthrow the system. Before they fight, an alternative solution surfaces: let's create humans to do the work! The celebration of the deal doesn't last long, however, because the pesky humans grow too noisy for the gods' taste and most are destroyed in an epic flood (thank God "loud Americans" backpacking through Europe haven't yet suffered the same fate). In these and other origin stories, gods must do battle with one another, must work to subdue the stuff of creation and secure their place as supreme.

This sort of hierarchical battling for power finds no place in the Genesis account. We don't have a story about how God won the right to take up space. The text assumes God's deity, God's sovereignty, God's agency. And when God creates, it's through an invitation to the stuff of creation itself to take up space and become more, bigger, full.

If we're honest, I think most would admit we tend to live shouting a hearty "thanks but no thanks!" to that invitation. It's an interesting proposal, really, but who can resist the million other narratives telling us to stay small? To be quiet? To take up as little space as possible? These stories are suffocatingly restrictive, but there's not much time or energy to assess that when you're staring at the cellulite on your thighs or the number on the scale. When you're in a room of power-brokers who want you to keep quiet, look pretty, and be grateful you're in the room at all. When your sex or color or orientation or accent or body are "wrong."

The restrictions feel like a necessary sacrifice to the gods, an offering to the deities who are busy battling it out for first place. Perhaps if I can stay small and silent enough, they'll forget that I'm here and I can quietly back away in peace while they feast on my offering.

Bullshit. All of it.

Your origin story centers on a God who from "the beginning" has been inviting you and me and all of creation to take up our space in the cosmos. She has never been tempted by the myth of scarcity, busy fighting battles for power and status among the gods. She has never been an angry homeowner, patrolling who walks her neighborhood. She has never been a dictator, threatened by the power and agency of others. She is and always has been a Creator—like a gardener, hands dirty in the mud, planting seeds and whispering in their ear about their capacity for growth within. Like a painter, calling forth the inspiration within her and delightedly watching it come to life on the canvas. Like a potter at the wheel, pulling the walls of clay upward so it can stretch into the vessel it was always made to be.

Since its very inception, the whole cosmos has been getting bigger; for as long as humans have drawn breath, we've been trying to contain it. We've erected systems to control creation and narratives to justify it. While Creator has looked at all she's made and called it "good," we've developed methods of determining who and what really deserves that designation, thank you very much. Like the capricious gods in other creation accounts, we've lived with violence at the center of our worlds, while the Creator, barefoot in the garden, whispers gently to the blades of grass, "Grow! Grow!"

On the days when whatever peace I've made with my thick thighs feels like a tenuous ceasefire on the verge of collapse, when I'm tempted to go small in body and spirit, I close my eyes and imagine I'm in a garden. I sense the lush grass beneath my feet and give way to the grounding energy rooting me to the earth. I exhale what toxic air remains within. I inhale the same pure air God breathed into my nostrils when I first became a living being. I remember my origin story, where Creator formed humans from the dust of the ground and called us "very good."

I see the dirt, the dust, the clay at my feet and remember, "This is the stuff I'm made of." And I find Creator there, in a small studio tucked away in the corner of the garden. She's huddled over a pottery wheel, once again playing in the clay. I observe her—the coarse graying curls that dance around her face and down her back, loose and wild; the earth tones filling the space around her; her jewelry and dress decorating her body and illuminating her spirit; the fullness and beauty of her frame. I feel alive in the creative energy, the hum of excited anticipation. I feel at peace in the calm, a quiet and contented stillness.

She looks up from her work and calls for me to sit with her, her voice textured like a massive rock face worn smooth by a steady stream. I think to myself, "Now I know why the sun burst forth at the mere sound of her voice summoning it to life. Now I know why it feels no shame in taking up its space." I watch her creative, expansive energy pulling the clay up from the wheel and into fuller form, feeling the same creative, expansive energy course through my veins.

I linger there, and I watch. When she looks at me, I can't help but speak.

"I want to be like you," I tell her.

"You are," she says.

7

God Is Seamstress

When our wounds cease to be a source of shame and become a source of healing, we have become wounded healers.

—Henri Nouwen

Healing does not mean going back to the way things were before, but rather allowing what is now to move us closer to God.

—Ram Das

See, I am making all things new.

—Revelation 21:5

In an upstairs bonus room just north of Nashville, my friend Diedre sits at her sewing machine. She's making a quilt for Christmas, with red and green cloth strips lying in tidy piles. She's been at this piece for months; she's been in her sewing room for decades.

Her first project was in a high school home economics class: a blush pink jacket with a matching pencil skirt. At nineteen she married Franklin, was pregnant soon after, and with the sewing machine she received as a wedding gift, she began stitching together maternity clothes for her expanding body. Soon she was creating clothes for her first daughter, and then another.

With every season, new pieces were needed: play clothes for the girls that they quickly grew out of; prom dresses in perfect 1980s style with metallic teal print and a mound of fabric at the shoulders; a lace wedding dress with hand-stitched beadwork; custom Halloween costumes for her grandkids; a baby blanket for her first great-grandchild.

When her twenty-year-old grandson comes home for the weekend from college with a tear in his favorite pants, she sits once again at her sewing machine, sewing a strip of cloth to join together frayed fabric. I admire her, admire her commitment to this craft that has been both necessity and hobby, labor and delight. Her hands have held fabric and pieced together thread to clothe her family for generations.

Long before Diedre tried her hand at sewing, she was a little girl in a chaotic home. Her parents had survived the Great Depression and recalled with pain the rations, the hunger. Her father was sent to fight in World War II, his own mother serving on the draft board that called his number. He didn't talk much about his experiences in war, though their effect was clear.

Two decades later, after serving in Vietnam, he came home and didn't leave his room for two years. He drank heavily. He erupted in anger at a moment's notice. He threw dinner plates at the wall. And he beat his wife. When Diedre's older brother would step in to protect his mom, father and son would fight in the living room until finally, when he was sixteen, her brother won the fight. Her dad sat dazed and bloody. Her brother crawled into the corner and sobbed.

Diedre's mother worked full time and had to provide for four children, knowing her husband could never be counted on to bring his paycheck home. She was a harsh woman, never a soft place to land. She pitted the children against one another and stirred tensions like a boiling pot. When Diedre graduated high school, the first one in her family to do so, no one attended the ceremony.

By the age of four, Diedre had already developed a way to cope in the midst of the chaos. As soon as the shouting and violence would erupt, she'd slip down the hallway and hide in her room. It was the only place she felt a measure of safety. As long as she could remain hidden, she could stay under the radar and avoid the worst of things. When the dust eventually settled and there was a lull in the storm, she would extend her head out the bedroom door, checking left and right to see if it was finally safe to come out.

She left home at seventeen, trekking from Kansas to New York, Florida to Washington, but she never stopped hiding. Even after marrying Franklin and starting a new life, a new family, she methodically withheld parts of herself in order to feel safe.

Decades into a successful career, she still wouldn't speak up when a supervisor's decisions impacted her well-being. At home, she withdrew into her sewing room when she needed to feel safe and be alone. When surrounded by other people, she could retreat internally, hiding inside a walled-off space within where she could hide in safety. A four-year-old's coping mechanism became a way of life.

Humans have been hiding since the very beginning. The third chapter of Genesis tells a story of Adam and Eve, the first two humans made by God and placed in a garden perfectly suited for their flourishing. As I heard it growing up, the story goes that these two humans disobeyed God, thus rendering the entire human race inherently sinful from that moment forward. This is why, when my girls first learned to say no and began exclaiming it like a badge of honor, people said things like, "Look at that sin nature at work, even at such a young age."

Christians say a lot of weird things, some of which is in fact beautiful and true and some of which drives me nuts. File the toddlers-with-a-sinful-nature label in the latter category for me, please. I'm not saying toddlers aren't crazy, or that they aren't hell bent on destroying the shred of sanity you managed to retain after the newborn phase. I'm saying that what some categorize as sin is sometimes better understood as a natural, normal, adaptive, and even healthy developmental process.

But hammers see nails everywhere, and ever since the fourth century when St. Augustine told us that the human condition is rooted in "original sin," we've gone on believing that humans are born sinful. I don't wax romantic when it comes to humanity's capacity for atrocity.

I was seven when I read *The Diary of Anne Frank* and visited Dachau, the first Nazi concentration camp. The last century alone saw more persons killed in war than in the combined nineteen before that. Despite our beloved notions of progress, we've been moving *in* the direction of the A-bomb, genocide, and ecological disaster, not *away from* them. It's not much of a stretch to see why many view Genesis 3 as explaining humanity's so-called fall and subsequent penchant for sin.

It's just that as I've sat with women experiencing incarceration inside prisons, as I've sat with women who have survived rape and assault, as I look at my own life, I've discovered a different telling of the story that squares with embodied reality in a way the traditional telling never has.

Adam and Eve are described as the first humans, placed in an idyllic garden with lush vegetation and ample sources of fresh water. Born of dust, they exist in a harmonious state with nature. They are like children, fresh to the world and full of wonder at its possibilities. It's this vulnerability that the serpent exploits. Readers familiar with the story know to expect the worst from this talking snake, but not Eve. Her assumptions about others, about the world, are good. Trust is assumed and freely given.

The serpent finds the woman and begins to expose her innocence to foul air. Cunningly, he poses questions that throw her mind into confusion and cast doubt on what she's previously known. Her desires are called into question, and she wonders what it is she wants and doesn't want. She loses trust in her own sensibilities, in her notions of God and self. Ultimately, the man and the woman eat the fruit held before them, and in an instant, everything changes. "Then the eyes of both were opened, and they knew that they were naked" (Gen. 3:7a).

This is an earth-shattering experience for the two humans, a we-can-never-go-back-to-before moment, a line drawn in the sand between what was and what is now. Suddenly their eyes are open to see everything differently, including themselves. And what they notice first is their nakedness. They've always been naked but somehow, it didn't matter, it didn't factor in. It's not that they feel differently about their nakedness now, it's that until this single moment in time they never knew to feel anything about it at all. It just was. This new awareness is devastating, their first encounter with shame. They frantically gather fig leaves and piece together crude garments to cover themselves and limit their exposure. And when God calls out for them—like my friend Diedre, like every human who has come after them—they hide.

A remarkable amount of energy has been spent debating whether this story, these texts, offer historical, scientific accounts. People want to know if it *really happened*. What is far more interesting to me is the indisputable reality that this story *happens*. It is the story of every human being who has entered the world in pure vulnerability and innocence, exploited by people and systems and powers, deceived by others with lustful, greedy motivations who themselves began in vulnerability and innocence.

To be a human being is to experience trauma, the kind that throws open the world in a new and haunting relief where we see ourselves through the lens of shame. Trauma takes every manner of overt and subtle form. Sometimes we can find the point on the map where the road suddenly diverged; sometimes it's in our bodies and we search without clear direction for its origin.

Regardless of trauma's form, our response often resembles that of the first humans, hurriedly gathering fig leaves to hide ourselves behind. With thread and needle we crudely piece together a garment of mechanisms that allow us to cope with the pain, the fear, the ache. We seek out a place to hide in bottles and pills and bars and bedrooms, in degrees and accolades and podiums and microphones, in sex and adventure and pleasure and thrill, in obscurity and silence and withdrawal and isolation.

You can fashion a suit of fig leaves in just about any style, but no trend can escape the brutal truth that the very clothing we hide behind is the very clothing that becomes our new trauma. Fig leaves contain a chemical compound that reacts with human skin, causing irritation, redness, blisters, swollen tissue, infection, and severe burns.

Experienced gardeners know to handle them with exceptional care. But to the average eye, the leaves' danger is invisible. The thoughts and behaviors and habits we form to cope with our pain become themselves a new form of pain, and the cycle of trauma continues.

When the first humans feel shame, when they long for the innocence now lost, they do the best they can with what they have. They sew loincloths from fig leaves, and they hide. This could have been the end of the story, humanity forever cursed to navigate the cycles of trauma, pain, hiding, and shame.

But God the Seamstress won't allow it. She walks through the garden calling out for the humans until she finds them.

"We were afraid because we're naked, so we hid," they say.

"Who told you that you were naked?" she asks (Gen. 3:10–11).

She gets to work making new clothes for the humans, ones that wrap their bodies lovingly with care rather than inflict wounds on their tender flesh. And with thread and needle in hand she sets out to begin a new tapestry that will lead to their healing, and to the healing of the universe.

A year ago, I sat in a classroom inside the Tennessee Prison for Women, teaching an undergraduate course in spiritual disciplines. Half of the women were "inside students," incarcerated in the prison, and the other half were "outside students," traditional undergrads who visited the prison once a week for class. On the one hand, there were obvious differences between the two groups, but on the other hand, their stories often bore remarkable resemblance.

Eighty percent of the students had endured sexual abuse, and every one of them could recall the moment they first became aware of their nakedness. Wounded humans are capable of inflicting unimaginable wounds on others. We respond from a place of pain and fear, lashing out with words and fists and weapons that scorch the earth around us. Sometimes we save the worst for ourselves, harming our own bodies before someone else has the chance to.

For the inside students, their reactions to pain and trauma were the kind that land one behind bars: theft, assault, drug use, murder. For the outside students, their reactions created an internal prison: eating disorders, perfectionism, workaholism, withdrawal. To sit among these women and share our stories, our wounds, our shame was to know without question that our trauma can become a dangerous weapon.

One winter afternoon as I sat in a cold cinder block room, prepared to speak on behalf of a student seeking parole, the cycle of trauma was so painfully clear it was all I could do to not weep. Years prior my student had shot her husband in attempted murder. But long before she pulled the trigger, she was the victim.

Her home was abusive and violent. She was groomed by an uncle who sexually assaulted her on a regular basis. And she left home at an early age, adamant that she never again would find herself so vulnerable. When she met her husband, he was battling his own demons, having served in a war that demanded he fight and kill. When the two married, their collective trauma fused to create a volatile home. He shouted and threatened her, mocking her belief that she might deserve something better. They had two sons together, raising them the best they knew how as they grappled with their own troubled childhood.

Finally, having endured enough of her husband's taunts and manipulation, she devised a plan to kill him. The bullet left him paralyzed, left their sons without a mother, left her aging mother-in-law to manage caring for everyone. I listened as the family wept, detailing the difficulties they had endured. I listened to my student's husband, bound to a wheelchair, acknowledging his harmful behavior that drove his wife to madness. I listened as my student pleaded with the parole board to grant her request so she wouldn't have to miss another day of her sons' lives. And I listened to the parole board, video conferencing in from another location, debating the fate of this family.

When the hearing was over, I walked to my car feeling a consuming heaviness. "My God, what does healing look like here?" I wondered. "And are we insane to ever believe it's possible?"

If we were to peel back the curtain and see into the layers of the world's gravest injustices, the world's most complex conflicts, it would look something like the tangled web of trauma I witnessed that day inside the prison. We would see the violent wars and death-dealing weapons and dehumanizing systems and structural oppression and crippling poverty and environmental devastation, yes. But we would also see the traumatized individuals sewing death and destruction into the fabric of the universe as they battle their deepest wounds, keeping the whole, hellish cycle in motion.

It's all so overwhelming that honestly, the fact that any of us gets out of bed in the morning feels miraculous. Some days, I struggle to believe that it could ever be otherwise, that this impossible mess is all we have and that it may very well lead to the entire world's demise.

But when I choose not to look away from the pain but instead look at the very heart of it, I see God the Seamstress in her sewing room, taking the pieces of violence and scraps of oppression and fragments of suffering and sewing them together in a new tapestry, the fabric of the universe made new. What to my eyes looks like an irreparable mess, a colossal shitstorm of hurt and pain and violence and death, to her eyes looks different. She somehow believes that healing is possible, and she sets out to make it so.

Some days, this dogged belief that the universe is moving toward ultimate healing is the only thing that keeps me going. Other days it feels like the most foolish of dreams. But whatever belief looks like for me on any given day, it seems to me that humans have a choice: we can keep pulling at the seams and tearing at the fabric, or we can pick up a needle and thread and learn how to sew.

In northern Iraq sits a refugee village housing Syrian families who fled a civil war, now raging for more than a decade. They sought shelter in a land torn apart by its own crises, the result of imported war and homegrown terrorism. When my colleagues at Preemptive Love[1] began working in this camp, they listened to the families' stories of lives turned upside down by violence and conflict. They heard about life before the war, how these refugees had once raised their families and farmed lush fields and invested in their communities.

Now here the families sat, in a one-room tent with a few basic necessities, trying to imagine how a better world could ever be. My colleagues are the kind of people who have an enormous capacity to imagine that better world and a resolute commitment to building it. The efforts began small in a nearby town where Yazidi women, targeted mercilessly by ISIS, learned how to make soap.

Soon a similar program sprang up with Israeli and Palestinian women working in a co-op sewing peace dolls—symbols of their persistent belief that despite all the evidence to the contrary, a different world is possible.

Our team drew on the successes of these programs, how they helped women brutalized by war and rape and loss become agents in their own lives once again. They taught women how to make candles and invited women with sewing and crocheting skills to join the circle. The program grew and the women began to come alive, but pouring hot wax and working with sharp needles in the middle of their cramped tents proved dangerous for their families. So the team set out to renovate a vacant building on site, turning it from a neglected room full of spiders and scorpions into a stunning space streaming with light where women makers can ply their crafts together.

They gather each day to create goods that are sold in the international market, earning them a fair wage and desperately needed income. They sew tea towels, knit children's toys, throw pottery, form bars of soap, and make candles. Their children play in the room next door, a safe place to experience some of the innocence and wonder that war stole from them. And each afternoon, the women take time for tea and talk about their lives with one another, remembering the past and imagining a future.

We can respond in a million ways to deep trauma. We can succumb to grief. We can pretend everything's fine. We can seek vengeance. We can isolate and hide. We can lash out. We can self-harm. We can chase egoic pursuits. We can put our hand to the wheel and spin it with all we've got, keeping the horrific cycle in nauseating motion. All of these responses make sense and none of us is above them.

But somehow, despite all the odds, we have a capacity for something else: an ability to lean into our deepest pain, acknowledge the suffering we've endured and the suffering we've perpetuated, and set out to write a different ending to the story. We can take the needle and thread in our hands, gather the frayed fabric, and get to work creating something new. We can pull up a chair in God's sewing room, listening as she tells us about the first clothes she ever made and how she's been coming to her sewing room ever since.

My friend Diedre is doing this kind of work. Like the four-year-old girl standing in her bedroom doorway, peeking into the hallway to discern whether it was safe to come out, safe to be vulnerable and exposed, she's begun tiptoeing out of hiding. She's thanked her fig leaves for helping her survive, and she's sewing garments suitable for her new season. She's pursuing training on how to hold space for people, how to listen well and ask thoughtful questions and help others feel safe in ways she never did. She's inviting other women to join her in her upstairs sewing room, not to work with fabric but to share their stories. She's creating space for women to bring their souls into free speech, even as she risks doing the same. Surrounded by quilts and pattern books, Diedre is discovering the utter holiness of this space.

Maybe, when the quilt of the universe is complete, when the threads have been stitched together to hold us all in and bind the tears in the fabric, we will gather in God's sewing room. We'll talk about our stories as we find them woven into the tapestry, interconnected with everyone else's. We'll remember our ways of hiding, numbing out, self-medicating, how we tore holes in the fabric of others' lives as we sought to make sense of the tears in our own.

And the God who is Seamstress will gather the quilt in her hands—the hands that have faithfully tended to it from the very beginning—and she'll wrap us up in healing.

God Is Mother

Can a woman forget her nursing child,
    or show no compassion for the child of her womb?
Even these may forget,
    yet I will not forget you.

                               —Isaiah 49:15

my
mother
was
my first country
the first place I ever lived.

                              —Nayyirah Waheed

Between the awkwardness of puberty and bad dressing room lighting, chronic illnesses and constant changes, youth group modesty talks and ceaseless dieting commercials, it is no easy thing to have a body. This suit of skin and bones and muscles and nerves—it's a wild existence even on the best of days. So we manage to find all manner of ways to disconnect from our own bodies. We begin to live in our heads, where it feels safer, until an experience comes along—a worrying diagnosis, a devastating injury, a midlife change—and suddenly we're thrust away from mental abstractions and back into the physicality of our bodies.

For me, motherhood was that experience, a wide-open invitation to embrace embodiment. I could not have foreseen all the countless ways that, from the first pangs of childbirth up until this very day, my body would be called upon to give and nurture life. Motherhood shifted me into a new season where I no longer back away from a baby's vomit but cup my hand in hopes of catching it. I wipe noses and butts and do not shudder at either. And through the days and nights of months and years, through cracked nipples and sheer exhaustion, I offer my body to my daughters over, and over, and over again.

There is no room for abstraction here, no time for romanticizing love or even reflecting on what I feel for my girls. There is only a precious little one who is hungry or sick or tired, a body that needs to be tended to and a body that needs to do the tending.

Motherhood is as embodied an experience as you can get. This is what makes it so beautiful and so damn difficult. I've always seen myself as a strong woman and I still do, but there are countless moments where the effects of aching exhaustion and clogged milk ducts and sticky floors and the inability to remember the last time I peed in private come crashing in on me and I feel certain *this is it. This will be what kills me.*

A week or so after having my first daughter and becoming a mother, when I somehow managed to scrape together enough energy for a conscious, semi-lucid thought, I remembered that people always say the love you have for your child is unlike anything you've ever known. They describe themselves as "obsessed" and "instantly in love" with their minutes-old newborn. So I asked myself: *Is it true? Do I feel that about this baby?*

The truth was, I didn't. I loved her, of course, in the I-would-give-my-life-for-you-in-a-second sort of love, but not the I-feel-things-I've-never-felt-before kind (unless of course we were talking about that searing pain in my perineum). I loved her, but I didn't *know* her. We had only just met, and I knew that the coming weeks and months and years would be a continuous process of learning who she was and what she was like, and loving *that* person (and for the record, she is amazing).

As it turns out, my feelings—or lack thereof—didn't matter all that much. The very second Olive was born, she was placed on my bare chest, and together we lay there for two hours, skin to skin. Before I could develop a single emotion or articulate what I felt or process all that had just occurred, I loved my daughter with my body. I held her tight to my chest. I draped her in my arms. And despite having no real certainty about what I was doing, I nursed her. Just as I had nurtured her developing body with mine for nine interminably long months, now I nurtured her with my body once again.

Maybe some moms really feel an immediate, gushing, overwhelming sense of love for their child the moment they meet. But here's what I'm convinced is true for moms everywhere: we love our children even when we don't feel like it, even when we're frazzled, even when we can't remember how to carry on an adult conversation, even when we question if we're doing it right, even when our baby bites our nipples for the hundredth time, even when we've sacrificed so much of ourselves we are certain there's nothing left to offer. We love our children, not just with our heads or with our hearts. We love our children with our *bodies.*

At times, the image of God as Mother is rather uncomfortable for me. I know myself as a mother. I know that the pictures we look back on will show sweet and beautiful moments, and there are so many of those to capture. But I also know the times when I've yelled at a baby who won't stop crying, or I've felt resentment for how much I've had to give up in order to parent, or I think I'll die if I have to prepare one more snack, or I've angrily thrown a water bottle across the room and accidentally shattered a picture frame because my baby is on week three of a nap strike that was supposed to be (I assume) her first act of nonviolent resistance but for me has been anything but peaceful.

In these kinds of moments I think, "Oh God, I hope you are not like a mother, because *I'm* a mother and I absolutely have blown it. I am terrible at this. I am raging. I am spent."

Thankfully, motherhood does not allow for too much of this kind of reflection, because even in the midst of my guilt or sadness or desperation, my girls have needs. And so, once again, I stoop down and draw those little ones into my arms. I hold them against my chest. I stroke their hair and caress their faces. I bring them to my breast and I offer of my body again, and again, and again. I love them with my body so they can experience life in theirs.

I don't pretend to know all the emotions God feels, or if she gets frustrated with me, or if she thinks to herself, "If I have to say this one more time . . ." But I do know that God has loved me with God's body, and God has mothered us all along.

The Hebrew Scriptures begin with an image of God like a mother bird, hovering over her young (Gen. 1:2). Eventually the creation is spoken fully into being and brought to life but before any of that happens, the unformed, unordered, chaotic stuff of creation is looked after by the Spirit[1] of God who hovers over it like a mama bird brooding over her eggs, incubating them with her warmth and her presence.

Over and over, we are told in the Hebrew Scriptures that God had compassion on her people. The Hebrew word for "compassion," *rachamin*, comes from the root word *rechem*, meaning "womb." Like a mother, God held the people of Israel in her womb, nurturing them and holding compassion for them as her children. When the people—frightened like a baby suddenly unable to locate its mother in a room—wondered if indeed God saw them, if God would take care of them, she offered her assuring presence. She reminded them that, like a mama, she was no more able to forget them than a woman can forget the baby nursing at her breast (Isa. 49:15).

Sometimes the people of Israel acted like whiny toddlers, stomping around and shouting "no!" loud enough for the neighbors to hear. Sometimes they acted like angsty teenagers, eager to rebel against whatever stupid rules impinged on their freedom. Sometimes they acted like twenty-somethings starting out in life, blithely sure of themselves and their own individualized path. No matter the season, God offered promises of healing and restoration. She promised to be like a nursing mother to Israel, comforting those whiny, angsty, independent people like a mother offers comfort at her breast (Isa. 66:12–13).

Jesus embodied this kind of motherly compassion and care, continually moved by love for the people he taught and healed and served. In one poignant scene he stood over the city of Jerusalem and proclaimed his long-felt desire to gather the people under his arms like a mother hen gathers her young and holds them tight (Luke 13:34; Matt. 23:37).

I grew up on the beach and about as far away from a farm as one could get, but I know that instinct. I felt it in me even before my girls came to be, and I'll feel it in me when I'm ninety-five with children not much younger. I think Jesus felt it until the end too, because in his final hours, he gathered his friends together for a meal like a mama whose grown kids have returned home for Thanksgiving.

Despite zero assurances that his friends would love him or get things right or follow a single one of the things he taught them, he sat with them at a table. He took bread and broke it. He took wine and shared it. He told them that in a similar way, his body would be broken so that they could find healing and redemption and freedom in theirs.

A few days later, he took into his body all of the world's death and violence and evil, and from it brought forth life for all of creation, the very creation God had hovered over in the very beginning.

God has always loved us with God's body.

For several years I witnessed this kind of embodied love most clearly in a small, windowless room at the back of a church sanctuary designated for mamas. Each week during the service, a group of us would gather—first-time moms and moms with five kids and moms who had adopted children and moms who were fostering infants and moms who stayed home and moms who worked demanding jobs and moms who breastfed and moms who used formula.

We would find our spot on a rocking chair and for what felt like the millionth time, we offered our bodies to nourish the babies in our care. We were broken open like a Eucharistic feast, saying to our babies, "Take. Eat. This is my body, broken for you." As we loved our babies with our bodies—with our breasts and our hands and our laps and our hearts—together as mothers we would share Eucharist. In the very same moment of feasting on the body and blood of Christ that somehow brings life, our own bodies were being broken and poured out for our children. This tiny room was the richest space in which to both partake of and offer a meal, to give life and to receive it.

It is a beautiful and burdensome thing to be a mother, one who sustains and tends to life in the midst of a world wracked by death. As I prepare meals, I think of the countless people for whom fear and terror and violence are the food they eat and the wine they drink. As I soothe the cries of my little ones, I hear the cries of those haunted by loss and grief and death, crying out for peace, for healing, for justice. As I hold my girls close and let them melt into my embrace, I wish so badly I had arms and chest great enough to comfort all who need it. "Come here baby," I want to say. "Mama's got you."

But in these moments, I remember the mothers from the nursing room and mothers the world over who beautifully and tenderly and faithfully care for children, delivering and sustaining life in the midst of every imaginable challenge. I think of the mamas who hold the hand of their disabled adult child crossing the street, the mamas who change diapers and gently care for tender flesh, the mamas who drive four hours one way for their child to see a specialist each week, the mamas who cross deserts holding infants so they can know a life without violence, the mamas who prepare gluten-free meals for their food-sensitive toddler, the mamas who scrape together meals when resources are scant, the mamas who endlessly scrub floors and countertops so their family can have clean spaces, the mamas who labor in fields with babies strapped to their backs, the mamas who cover their children's ears so they don't hear the gunshots down the street, the mamas who prepare snacks for the soccer team, the mamas who gently bathe little ones even when they themselves haven't showered in days, the mamas who fit in their cancer treatment before picking up their kids from middle school, the mamas who fall to their knees every morning praying for their addict child to get sober, the mamas who attend class with a toddler on their lap, the mamas who braid hair and tell their babies how beautiful they are, the mamas who show up to yet another city council meeting demanding sufficient services for their child, the mamas who make birthday cakes to celebrate special days, the mamas who pump in airport bathrooms so their babies have milk, the mamas who stay up waiting to make sure their teenagers make it home safely, the mamas who make a home out of a tent in a refugee camp.

The world can be a dark and painful place, yes, but there are mamas nurturing life everywhere. And from the beginning, God has always been a mother—extending her arms outward to embrace her children, soothing our aching hearts, binding our deepest wounds, and inviting us to a table with ample food and drink for all.

Since becoming a mother my body has been called upon in all manner of ways to give and nurture life for my daughters. Sometimes, when I feel I cannot manage things another hour, when I feel anger or sadness or desperation or exhaustion, I image God as Mother and I pour my heart out to her in words and tears and moans. While I serve as my daughters' source of comfort and nourishment and safety, I seek these things in the safe bosom of the God who invites me to her chest, to hear her heartbeat and know that all shall be well, and all shall be well, and all manner of things shall be well.

As I sit with cracked nipples and leaking breasts, I see my God as one familiar with her body being broken on behalf of those she loves, with giving herself entirely so we might be fully alive. In a singular moment, I am both a reflection of this God to my daughters—body broken and poured out for them—and I am a distressed child needing this God's loving embrace.

Chapter 8

In the wee hours of the morning or in the late hours of a long day, when I am once again called on to care for a little one who knows no other means of recourse but to need me, I hold in my heart all of God's beloved children who desperately need the arms of a mother to wrap them up and cradle them close and whisper, "It's okay, baby. Mama's got you." As I love my daughters with my body, I find comfort in the God who loves her children with hers.

God Is Midwife

Listen to me, O house of Jacob,
    all the remnant of the house of Israel,
who have been borne by me from your birth,
    carried from the womb;
even to your old age I am [the one],
    even when you turn gray I will carry you.
I have made, and I will bear;
    I will carry and will save.

—Isaiah 46:3–4

The body is like Mary. Each of us has a Jesus, but so long as no pain appears, our Jesus is not born. If pain never comes, our Jesus goes back to his place of origin on the same secret path he had come, and we remain behind, deprived and without a share of him.

—Rumi

A lot of waiting goes on in hospitals. Waiting for results. Waiting for family to arrive. Waiting for the pain to subside. In labor and delivery wards, the waiting—like the women in it—is full and ripe and pregnant. The moment sits just on the edge of culmination, the collective holding together of childhood dreams of mothering and fears about getting it wrong and time spent trying to conceive and months of growing life within. To be witness to the exact moment when the waiting transitions to the present tense is so potent and surreal that it can almost pass you by.

I witnessed just such moments when, as an ill-prepared and energetic twenty-something, I began my career working with young women who found themselves unexpectedly pregnant. I was not much older than they were, yet somehow they invited me into what is perhaps the most vulnerable of experiences: childbirth.

As I tended to the hearts and spirits of these young women, seeking to offer them safe spaces wherein they could process all they held, I began to notice the midwives who tended to their bodies. Other medical professionals moved briskly, worked quickly, and acted professionally—often in response to an emergency or the threat of one—working *on* the women and their babies. But the midwives' care for laboring mothers was human in every good sense of the term. True to their title (midwife means "with woman"), they did not work on or around the mothers. They worked *with* them.

Most laboring mothers know instinctively that their bodies are capable of labor, the very bodies that formed and sustained life for nine months. But when contractions descend on the body like a wave of electric energy you can easily forget that your body is capable of anything but sensing unnerving pain.

It was this pain I feared most during my first pregnancy. For the first six or seven months I tried to avoid thinking too much about the pending process of labor and delivery. I told myself and everyone else that I didn't yet have the time or energy to give it much thought or begin preparation.

And this was true. I had papers to grade and lectures to write and nausea to keep at bay. But I also wanted very much to delay the point when finally I would have to face the reality that there was only one way this whole thing could end, and this baby eventually would have to make her way out. This suppression of my anxiety ended the moment my husband and I drove to our first birthing class.

I felt worse and worse the closer we got to the building. When we pulled into the parking lot, my once-hidden anxiety rushed up from wherever I had kept it in storage and threatened to undo me. My husband, as he often does, looked at me and asked what I was thinking. Damn him.

I spend an inordinate amount of energy keeping myself together and presenting well to others. When something threatens that very tightly monitored ecosystem it is threat to the highest degree. Seeking to maintain at least some sense of composure, I told him through tears that I was scared.

Actually, I was terrified. I had gotten myself into a situation from which I had no means of escape, and I had only one option: face the pain and do this thing. Having no time to process any of what I had revealed to my husband and to myself, we walked into the classroom. Willing my tears to keep their mouth shut, I resolved that I could hold it all together for the next two hours.

My birthing coach said no. Actually, what she said to every other woman in the room in the get-to-know-you exercise was a series of benign and gentle and even adorable questions: "Where are you from?" "When are you due?" "What color are you painting the nursery?" "Have you decided on a name?" But she zeroed in on me in all of my suppression and she went for the jugular: "What do you fear most about labor?" Damn her.

Her question, and my subsequent preparation for childbirth, forced me out of my head—where I tend to live—and into my body, the vessel that was miraculously creating life within and would soon be called upon to bravely deliver that life into the world. This shift proved essential. We can—and often do—live our lives seeking to escape our bodies, to spiritualize reality and divide the world into categories of spirit and matter, sacred and secular. But when that first contraction moves through your body like a shockwave, all of the spiritualizing in the world cannot move a baby one inch through the birth canal.

This is the *body's* work, and there is no room for abstraction in it. There is only the body, and movement, and blood, and groans, and pain, and beauty. Laboring life into the world is the work of the body. And joining women in that labor is the work of midwives.

When I first found out I was pregnant, I knew immediately that I wanted to deliver with midwives. Fortunately for me, a brand-new birthing center had opened in Nashville just months before, and it was nicer than any hotel I had ever stayed in. The waiting areas were set up like a living room, with hot tea on the counter and Ella Fitzgerald in the speakers. The delivery rooms looked like bedroom suites with plush white linens and fancy wallpaper. The tub in the corner sat in front of wide windows, letting in loads of natural light, and the toilet seat was warmed to a perfect temperature (who knew this was possible?).

These amenities, while luxurious, were chosen to communicate not sophistication but humanization. Every aspect of the birthing center was designed to affirm a basic truth to pregnant women: pregnancy, labor, and delivery are normal human processes (as normal as sitting comfortably in your own bedroom).

On the one hand, this seems an expensive way to make an incredibly obvious point. But in an age and culture where birth has been systematized in countless ways—viewing women's bodies as cogs in a mechanical, industrialized process—it is often the simplest of pronouncements that are the most profound. For centuries, births took place in homes, attended to by other women, who themselves had delivered babies in their homes, attended to by other women.

Too often, modern delivery wards—full of incredibly valuable, life-saving tools and technology to assist in emergencies—can feel cold, clinical, sterile. The birthing center was warm, comfortable. But no amount of carefully chosen pillows and light fixtures can sufficiently create a culture of safety and affirmation. That came from the midwives.

From my first prenatal appointment to my final postpartum checkup, these women empowered me—with their words, their actions, their presence. They reminded me that my body was capable of creating and delivering a baby, that pain was part but not the whole of the process, that I had all I needed to successfully do what was required. And it was that sense of empowerment that finally disrupted my fears and anxiety and prepared me for the birth of my daughter, and eventually another.

I remembered something I'd read in midwife-pioneer Ina May Gaskin's book, *Guide to Childbirth*. She explores the different kinds of pain we feel and how we respond to them. When a knife cuts your hand and blood begins to bubble to the surface, the pain you feel is a response telling you something is wrong, and that is a gift. But the pain is still real, so you seek to address or numb or alleviate it.

But in childbirth, Gaskin states, the pain you feel is not your body's way of telling you something is wrong. It is your body telling you that everything is right on track, that it's doing what it needs to do, that each contraction is *purposeful* and is leading you closer and closer to the moment where new life emerges. This shift in perspective proved essential for me, because regardless of whatever enlightened thoughts you hold toward childbirth, that shit still hurts.

When the contractions came like waves, one after another, I had to learn how to ride those waves. I had to reject every one of my normal tendencies to grasp control or insulate myself from pain or numb all discomfort. I had to submit *to my own body*, because it knew better than I did. Somehow, in a way I cannot explain, I simply entered into the process that was unfolding within and around and through me. I rode the waves, and I felt the pain, and I let my body do its work.

But I did not do this alone. My midwife, Heather, joined me in this process. True to every act of empowerment prior to my labor, she continued to affirm my ability to give birth, telling me how great I was doing and how proud she was, filling up the tub with warm water and placing pressure on my back to provide some relief. It was her presence with me that mattered most, and not just *that* she was present but *how*.

Pregnant women generally enter into labor and delivery with little prior experience, and even women who have several children only have those two or three births from which to draw insight and perspective. This can sometimes make small things feel enormously alarming or significant. But midwives do all of their work having attended hundreds and sometimes thousands of prior births, holding that collective set of stories and experiences with them as they attend to the laboring woman before them. Because of this, they can remain calm, and composed, and intentional, and present.

Heather was present to me in the most reassuring and affirming of ways. Her very spirit seemed to hold out this collection of stories she carried, the women she had served and the beautiful babies she had helped deliver. As I labored, it was as if all of those women and babies were also present in the room, affirming that I had within me what I needed to join their ranks. Just as Heather drew on her experience, I drew from this community, and together we labored.

And labored. And labored. And labored some more. For twenty-four hours, to be exact—about twenty more than I had hoped for. There were plenty of moments in the midst of incredible pain where, had I some magical option to speed things along, I gladly would have taken that pill or pushed that button or drank that potion. But there is no rushing in labor. There is the labor, and there is the waiting.

My body knew this, and it kept working through the process one contraction at a time. My midwife knew this too. She never sought to rush the process, not for one second. She sat with me on the bed and by the tub and on the floor and next to the birthing stool, and she labored with me.

Had I ever sensed that she was in a hurry, that she wanted things to happen more quickly, I would have frozen. Midwives can tell you countless stories of what happens to a woman's body when someone—medical professional, partner, friend—in the delivery room is anxious or negative or hurried. The woman's body literally closes up, stalls out, halts the process. The body senses threat and responds, and when your body is assessing fight or flight modes, it doesn't have much energy to devote to working a baby through a birth canal. It takes careful, attentive, affirming energy to support and nurture the body's laboring process, the kind that my midwife offered. Every time

I wanted the pain to stop and for the whole thing to be over, I heard Heather whisper in my ear, "You're doing so great, mama."

I had hoped to be more presentable during labor, able to gently smile for a photo like those women on Instagram. But in reality, I was a naked mess, sweating profusely and groaning in pain. There was nothing covered or hidden or presentable about that process. I was wide open, on display, having the most primal of experiences in the most primal of ways. Humans generally don't prefer being totally naked in front of other humans (or sometimes even in front of our own selves). Our bodies are often the site of our deepest trauma and we hold our wounds in our flesh, terrified of being hurt or seen or exposed. Add to this the insecurities about our weight or the shape of our nose or that precariously positioned mole, and being naked is literally and figuratively our nightmare.

When we muster all bravery and risk being so vulnerable as to be naked in front of another human being—whether physically naked in sex or metaphorically naked in our being transparent and honest—the worst possible response from another person would be to shame us for it. Heather sat with me—a naked, vulnerable, writhing woman in labor, breasts and genitalia and fear all exposed—and once again she whispered, "You're doing so great, mama." There was no shaming. There was no judgment. There was only the gift of full, affirming presence. This is what midwives do. This is who they are. And it is why I image God as Midwife.

The human life is full of crippling uncertainties, devastating losses, unsettling disruptions, and bone-chilling pain. Sometimes, a birthing experience itself becomes the source of a family's deepest pain. Sometimes a baby doesn't survive or a mother's delivery is full of trauma and disappointment.[1] More often than not, in seasons of deep pain, we ask questions about why God is doing this to us or what lesson we're supposed to learn from it or what we've done wrong. Or we turn on the most uplifting—if not obnoxious—inspirational music and literally try to drown out the nagging pain that keeps surfacing, telling ourselves to keep a positive outlook and praise God in the storm, ad nauseam.

In either case, it seems to me that we miss it. We miss the reality that brokenness is part of the human experience, and that God does not orchestrate who gets cancer and who gets a good parking spot. Sometimes, life is just shitty.

Sometimes, things don't make sense. We endure pain that overwhelms our body like a contraction, seizing our attention and sanity. If we were honest, most of our prayers in times like these are something like the unrealistic (but nonetheless entertaining) labor scenes in movies, where exhausted mothers shriek in pain and demand the doctor give them drugs. We feel pain and we want it gone. And there's no shame in this. Few people *enjoy* pain.

But sometimes we need to be reminded that, like a contraction, this pain has movement and it won't last forever. If we allow it to, it can take us somewhere and birth something in us.

Like a midwife, God comes alongside of us in our most vulnerable of experiences where we had every intention of being composed and camera ready, but in reality we're a naked mess writhing on the floor, sweat burning our eyes, feeling like we can't endure another moment—and God whispers, "You're doing so good, mama." At the point we feel the weakest or the most vulnerable or the most afraid, God is most present, attentive to us, affirming us.

Labor is a messy process, in every possible way, but midwives like God don't shy away. Midwives enter into the mess, never once shaming the woman for her fear or her cries or her nakedness. And at the same time, midwives remind you that this pain will not kill you, it won't do you in and end you. Sensing pain doesn't always mean things have gone badly or that something is wrong. Sometimes it just means you're a human having a human experience, as human as giving birth. Midwives remind you that the pain you're feeling has the power to bring forward new life, life you never could have dreamed up in a million years.

Sometimes I think we envision God as this great cosmic being who will take all of our pain and make it all easier. But even the most skilled and caring midwife cannot perform a single second of the woman's labor. She cannot take over and do the work. The work is within the woman to do, to experience. The midwife joins the woman in this experience, comes alongside and mirrors the woman's breathing, the pulsating rhythms of her body, so that somehow, they labor together.

This kind of labor, this kind of surrender to pain and all of its possibilities, takes time. I'd much prefer to keep a quick pace in life with my hands on the reins at all times, but I lost the option for control the second I stepped into the birthing room. And while death itself generally feels preferable to me than losing control, somehow the experience of labor helped me release my felt need to see, understand, and control everything and be fully present in my body which was already doing good work.

That work took time. It always does. There have been so many difficult seasons in life when I wished for nothing more than the ability to snap my fingers and move on to the next. In those seasons, God midwifed me, reminding me that the pain was real but would not overtake me, that I had all I needed within, that this movement was purposeful and was taking me somewhere, that ultimately, new life was being born.

The final phase of active labor, called transition, is the most difficult. The pain becomes overwhelming, the body literally feeling as though it were on fire. It becomes extraordinarily difficult to stay in the rhythms of breathing and pushing, breathing and pushing. It feels like failure, like regression, like the end.

As individuals, as communities, as a world, we know these transition moments. We are in a great transition even now, where the darkness abounds and the pain feels unbearable. But as Sikh activist Valarie Kaur asks, "What if this darkness is not the darkness of the tomb but the darkness of the womb?"[2] What if we are in "one long labor"? What if we could surrender to the Force of Life within and around us, guiding our spirits and bodies with ancient, primal wisdom?

What if we could breathe—acknowledging our worth and that of our neighbors—and push—joining the great community of laborers who have insisted that new life can emerge from pain? What if we entered fully into what's taking place, joining our own selves to be present in the labor, to surrender to the movement and energy that's carrying us forward, to risk the pain of labor and feel the full weight of it because we know—somehow, in some way—it is leading to life?

When we do, there is no one better to guide new life into the world than the God who is Midwife.

God Is Hostess

On this mountain the Lord of hosts will
make for all peoples
    a feast of rich food, a feast of well-aged wines,
    of rich food filled with marrow, of well-aged wines
       strained clear.

—Isaiah 25:6

We have all known the long loneliness and we have learned
that the only solution is love and that love comes with
community.

—Dorothy Day

I attended my first church camp when I was seven. A decade later I
would meet my husband at a church camp, but on this occasion, I only
had eyes for one man: the camp chef. His name was Ed, as I recall,
and he dished out food that was mostly edible—which, by camp food
standards, deserves a nod from James Beard. Ed was the kind of chef
who stands by the food line as people make their plates—whether to
delight in their enjoyment or to critique their simple palettes, I don't
know. But Ed was kind and seemed genuinely pleased that I enjoyed
what he prepared.

When my friend and his dad dropped me off at home at the end of the week, my friend boasted a shiny new medal he had earned at camp with the words "Best Christian Testimony" engraved in deep gold. How one determines this for prepubescent seven-year-olds, I have no idea, but nonetheless, there it was: recognition of his noble Christian character. His dad, not wanting me to feel left out or overlooked, made sure my parents knew that I too had been recognized for an accomplishment. They looked at me proudly and with excitement, waiting to hear what award I had received. I pulled that medal out of my bag full of dirty laundry and modest swimwear and held it out for all eyes to see: "Best Eater."

It was my mom's fault, really. She was always the kind to cook big meals and make sure that if a small tribe of nomads just happened to show up on our doorstep for dinner, there would be plenty of food to go around. I hated to stay for dinner at some of my—usually very skinny—friends' houses because their families offered such stingy portions for meals and I thought, *Who has time for this?! They're having third helpings at home.*

The trait is hereditary. My grandmother shows love in a million ways but my *favorite* has always been her cooking. She manages to create chewable, delicious love. Everything she makes is better than everything anyone else makes. And it's not just what she makes but *how* she makes it. As a kid I would hold up limp toast at breakfast and whine to my parents. "It's just that, when *Mema* butters toast, the knife makes a 'shh shh' sound, and it tastes better."

The way that woman cuts a banana is a work of art. It should be studied. The very best memories of childhood were when I got to have sleepovers at her house. I would lie in the dark guest room in the coziest bed imaginable watching Game Show Network until 3:00 a.m. And every night around eleven o'clock or midnight, Mema would tip-toe down the hallway to pop in and ask, "Would you like a barbecue turkey sandwich and chocolate milkshake?" Her instincts were a million times better than every one of those suckers trying to play *$25,000 Pyr-*

amid because somehow, yes, that is *exactly* what I was craving, Mema, and yes, that would be a delicious midnight snack. Thank you.

My family has always been full of generous table hosts. They never fail to create space for others to join in, to make sure that there is more than enough food (even at midnight) to go around. And I have always been the grateful, award-winning recipient.

Being raised by such generous hosts, I grew up believing that there was space for everyone at the table. No one was left out. The food was abundant and delicious and everyone was welcome to it.

I remember one of the first times I finally realized that not everyone hosts such generous tables for me.[1] I was in my first or second semester of grad school, learning Greek vocabulary and when the book of Matthew was probably written and plenty of other things I promptly forgot. Before class one day I asked another student about his experiences teaching Bible classes at a nearby school. I've always been drawn to teaching. It feels natural to me in a way that math and closed-toed shoes do not.

When he mentioned that a position was opening, I was thrilled. "This might be the open door I've been longing for," I thought. When he asked what I wanted to teach, I watched his face slowly turn in on itself as I told him my desire to teach Bible. He stammered an awkward response about how his school didn't allow women to teach co-ed Bible courses for students past the age of twelve, but that I could possibly teach a girls' class. In that moment, I felt my entire past crash into the stark reality of the present moment, and suddenly I knew: *There is not enough room at the table for me.*

In the years since that encounter I have bumped up against every single barrier erected within patriarchy to tell a woman, "You can go this far but no farther." I have been told I can teach classes about certain topics but not others. I have been allowed to preach a sermon but only if a man remained on the platform with me. I have had my sermons called "lessons" or "presentations" and my preaching sanitized to "teaching." I have had people walk out of the room when I stood up to preach. I've been told "thanks but no thanks" when I offered to preach while the dude-with-zero-training got to stand behind the pulpit. I've been told that my anger about all of this is off-putting. I have students eager to tell me of God's disapproval of who I am. I have been told I'm just after a personal agenda. I have been silenced.

Much more than my own painful encounters, I carry those of the women around me, friends and colleagues and students who daily collide with the same absurd barriers. I've listened to women who watch as their abuser is once again honored and given even greater authority while they are told their voice is too much. I've observed young girls' utter confusion when the cultural message they hear is "You can do anything!" and the church message they hear is "Just not here!" I've had seventy-year-old women cradle my face and beg me, "Please do not be silent. I have been silent my whole life. I hope you live with far more self-confidence as a woman than I ever have." I've listened to women colleagues describe the men students in their courses who refuse to make eye contact with them, demonstrating their clear disdain for having a woman Bible professor. I've held the tears of friends who weep for the pain of knowing in their bones they're meant to pastor others but who can't find a single church who will let them. I know of a woman with a PhD in biblical studies who was allowed to teach Sunday school classes only if a man was present, standing, and if she remained seated. And I've heard every one of these barriers defined as God's good plan for women.

My friend Sara tells the story of growing up in a small town in 1970s Arkansas. Her family being active members of a local congregation, she and her brothers would often play church. When they played house or pretended they were shopkeepers, she knew what to do and eagerly joined in the imaginative play. But when they played church, she implicitly knew that she could not contribute, that her brothers would take the parts of minister and elder, and that she was to sit quietly in the pew like any good church girl ought to. It didn't take long for her to get bored with this, so she would run off and play *Charlie's Angels* instead. By age five or six, Sara understood that the message of *Charlie's Angels* was somehow better news (or at least more empowering) than what she heard at church.

Within the church I've encountered plenty of tables with a meager spread and too few chairs. But the church by no means has a monopoly on stingy hosting customs. Cultures and political parties and country clubs and institutions do the very same.

Religiously inspired or not, to host tables where only certain kinds of people are welcome is to buy into the myth of scarcity that lurks behind virtually every cultural message we hear, like a stranger in a dark alley. We are told—craftily and with clever marketing techniques—that there is not enough to go around—not enough money or power or resources or citizenship or fame or whatever—so we ought to amass for ourselves all that we can and limit others' access. Our evolutionary impulses toward self-preservation get played like a musical instrument and we fall prey to its lulling sounds. And the church, capable of creating music far more beautiful than this, sets down its own hymnals and sings along with the toxic messages.

I would love to say that I have an ear always attuned to this song, ready to name it for the counterfeit that it is. But too often, I find myself humming along, internalizing the myths of scarcity and peering out from a front window like an over-zealous neighbor, watching and waiting for any sign of threat to my property. At the same time that I weep and wail against the injustices of stingy tables where women can't find a seat, I look at these sisters as competition. When they're invited to speak at a conference or their gifts are praised, when they're promoted or signed to a book deal, I'm afraid it's one less bite for me. And I'm so hungry for equitable, generous tables that I begin to believe the issue is a lack of resources rather than unjust systems ensuring only a few seats are available.

Each of the four gospels tells a familiar story about Jesus and his disciples being approached by crowds of people. Jesus had withdrawn to a quiet place with his closest friends, but even there the people seek him out like toddlers who refuse to let their mom pee in peace, wiggling their toes under the door and demanding Goldfish. Somehow,

Chapter 10

he has compassion on the crowds and moves among them, teaching them about the "kindom"[2] of God and healing the sick. As the day drags on, Jesus's disciples urge him to send the people away because night is coming and they would need to seek food and shelter (you have to give the toddlers their Goldfish eventually).

I imagine myself in this story. Immediately, I sense anxiety from seeing large crowds approaching, wondering how on earth to manage the situation. And *then* to realize they are hungry and there are no restaurants for miles? It's almost too much. I feel frantic and fearful and quickly shift into planning mode, determining the best option possible for getting these people fed and mitigating the damage.

I look at Jesus. And just as I am about to tell him the good news that I've got a plan and it will take some maneuvering but I think we can make it work, he smiles gently at me in a way that sees and affirms and identifies my ridiculousness but never invalidates or belittles or shames. It's quite a look. He walks over to me, places his hand lovingly on my chest and says, "This anxiety you feel is not from me. Let's find a different way." While the knots of tension slowly begin to unfurl in my gut, I watch as Jesus takes what seems to be insignificant at best in the face of a hungry crowd—five loaves of bread and two fish—and manages to create the kind of spread my family would be proud of.

In these encounters I see with clarity the ways I swallow whole every perceived threat of scarcity yet somehow never feel satiated. As I'm moved by the God Who Is Hostess to spit out these toxic tastes, I am moved by the same to call out every table that serves them, every unjust table host who sets small tables with only a few prized seats. I'm reminded of those who have even less access to the table than me, those whose color and class and sexual orientation and citizenship status and abilities make it hard—or even *impossible*—to pull up a seat. And I set out determining how to bust up this old table and create a new one fitting of a Generous Hostess.

Some days I feel energized to do this, energized *by* this work. But most days, I just feel weary. I just want to come home after a long day of school and find that my mom has been hard at work preparing a delicious dinner, a meal that will nourish and satisfy, a table spread far and wide with ample space for whoever may wish to join. What I often find instead are tersely written refrigerator notes explaining that, while it's sweet for my friends and me to stand in our worthiness and dignity, there's simply not enough room at the table for everyone, but if we're willing to stay in the pre-ordained spaces acceptable for our kind we can probably get along just fine.

And so, like a child who cannot count on home as being a safe place where she is seen and known and affirmed, a child who seeks belonging but is met instead with inhospitable spaces, I rush out to establish a name for myself. To erect my own sense of self by whatever means available. I try to make more of myself than I am to prove I'm worthy of being invited to dinner, or I shrink back and become small to demonstrate that I can be a polite and compliant guest. I walk into rooms with a radar scanning every possible interaction as one where I'll need to defend or prove myself. I analyze my performance like a biting critic, detailing every way I am not up to snuff. And I walk away hungry still.

Several years ago, I began training folks to become spiritual directors. What has always drawn me most to this ancient practice of spiritual direction is the ability to host a safe and welcoming space for someone, a space wherein they can bring their soul into speech without fear of judgment or critique or shame. I need these spaces, so I work to create them for others.

I was so eager to help multiply the number of folks who would hold these kinds of safe spaces open for others. Yet in the very space where I was teaching these budding directors how to be generous table hosts, some students were eager to let me know their discomfort with my being a woman. As I was trying to prepare a table, they pulled my chair right out from under me. There is no way to adequately measure the impact of this dynamic, the way it hangs on me like a lead vest.

After a particularly difficult day with these students, I drove home in tears, wanting for nothing more than to crawl into my bed and find that my Mema had made a barbecue turkey sandwich and a chocolate milkshake topped with extra sprinkles because she could tell I needed them. Even with 726 miles between us, I considered for a moment the possibility of driving home because I was so hungry for that kind of table.

Instead, I called my spiritual director and wept for every single time that people are made to feel less than, are told to be small and quiet, are conditioned to see themselves as anything less than the God-breathed miracle they are. I felt the anger in me surge like a wave, the hurt even more palpable yet. I wondered whether there will ever be a time when people don't have to navigate a world of inhospitable tables and stingy table hosts.

In the midst of my grief, I began to sense the God Who Is Hostess. I saw God as a Community of Three Persons seated around a table, like in Andrei Rublev's icon, *Trinity*. I was reminded that at this table, everyone is welcome, that this God is one who does not calculate how many spots are available but rather makes more space in her own self for others to join. I reflected on the dynamics of a God who exists as a Community of Hostesses, always creating and preparing hospitable spaces into which humanity can enter and be nourished and seen. There is no in-fighting among this God, no petty squabbles about who is more powerful and able to do what. There is equity and generosity and service and deference and rich hospitality. In my grief and frustration, I heard this Hostess say to me, "You will always have a seat at *this* table."

I felt the gaze of the Hostess and her invitation to me begin to melt the defenses I keep erect at all times. I felt her love overcoming my grief, her generosity speaking a better word to every myth of scarcity—the ones force-fed to me and the ones I willingly chew on.

At every table there is proper etiquette, appropriate ways of behaving and interacting. I never went to cotillion or charm school, but I know the basics (that scene in the dining room from *Titanic* has helped a lot). I've been sufficiently conditioned to know that, at a table or in a room, women are expected to take up only so much space. Sometimes this means we shrink back or don't share our opinion. Sometimes we remain quiet under the guise of politeness. And sometimes it means we starve ourselves lest our very bodies demand too much space.

Without fail, every semester in every class I teach, I have women students who apologize each time before asking a question. Girls are socialized into these patterns from an early age. And rather than serving as a beacon of good news, proclaiming a better word to women than this, too often the church serves the leftovers from the very same poisoned meal.

But at the table where God is Hostess, this kind of suffocating table etiquette is swallowed up in her generosity and hospitality. God never demands for her guests to become smaller. Rather, she makes space within her own self into which she invites creation, a table with room for everyone, a feast for us to eat with joy and gratitude. When God says, "You will always have a seat at this table," she doesn't just mean that she can possibly squeeze in one more seat at the end. She means that there is plenty of room, room for us to be fully present and fully ourselves, room for us to spread out and prop up our elbows and have second helpings and join in the conversation.

There are a million ways people have been excluded from tables, left off the guest list, restricted from partaking of the meal. Our gender, our sexuality, our religion, our race, our bodies—these are the exclusion criteria by which we've been told there's no room for us. But like my mother and my grandmother, God is a generous Hostess, always making space for us at her table. May we find our seat, may we eat our fill, and in our experience of rich hospitality may we make space in our own selves for others.

God Is Sexual Trauma Survivor

The study of trauma in sexual and domestic life becomes
legitimate only in a context that challenges the subordina-
tion of women and children.

—Judith Herman

i am not wounded
i am bleeding to life
we need a god who bleeds now
whose wounds are not the end of anything

—Ntozake Shange, "We Need a God Who Bleeds Now"

In 1984, the Cathedral Church of Saint John the Divine in New York
City displayed a small bronze sculpture above an altar. The four-
foot figure easily could have been overlooked in the church's 121,000
square feet, the sixth largest church in the world. But the controversy
it stirred outsized the massive cathedral's footprint.

The art piece was called "Christa," a small sculpture depicting a
naked woman in a crucified position—a female Christ figure. Immediately after its installment, the church received hate mail. People called
it blasphemous, offensive, abhorrent. The head of the church's diocese
at the time called it "theologically and historically indefensible,"[1] and
within just a few days it was taken down, packed up, and carried off.

The crucifixion is a common focal point in various art forms, but this piece struck a nerve in a way those often don't. It was the female body, breasts exposed, that for many could only be seen as pornographic. Edwina Sandys, the sculpture's creator, wanted to portray the suffering that women around the world endure. But for many observers it was simply out of the question to connect Jesus's crucifixion with female embodiment.

Much has changed since "Christa" made her debut in the mid-1980s. But the need for robust theological conversations about the traumas women endure—particularly sexual trauma—has not waned a bit.

I began my career working at a residential facility for young women. Some battled with eating disorders and were locked in a hopeless cycle of binging and purging or had starved themselves to a critical point. Some were severely depressed and anxious, seemingly unable to handle even basic daily tasks or interactions with others. Some harmed their own bodies because seeing the result—blood, scars, burns—helped release some of the enormous pain they carried. Some were pregnant and fifteen. Some had numbed themselves through drugs and alcohol and addictions of all kinds. Their struggles varied, but what was true for some 85 percent of the young women was that they had survived sexual abuse.

Some had hardly known a life without constant sexual abuse at the hands of a parent or caretaker. Others faced assault and harassment by middle school boys when they turned thirteen. Some had been brutally raped by a stranger, or a friend, or a partner. Some were the victims of organized sex trafficking rings that turned brutality into profit. The stories were horrifying. I felt equal parts deep grief at the sheer suffering they had endured and utter gratitude at their willingness to invite me into these parts of their stories. The work was hard, and it was holy.

It inspired my doctoral research. I continually found myself in two spaces: a residential facility full of trauma survivors, and an academic program full of ministers and scholars ill-equipped to care for these survivors in ways that didn't perpetuate further harm. I wanted to help my peers better understand the nature of sexual trauma and provide resources for them so that in their churches, their classrooms, and their homes they could provide desperately needed safe space for survivors. So I jumped headfirst into trauma theory.

It was only a century ago that scientists began delving into trauma in a formalized way. For much of the twentieth century, studies focused on men war veterans' post-combat experiences and the invisible but deep wounds that lingered. It wasn't until the 1970s—as women's liberation movements gained ground—that researchers realized the majority of people battling post-traumatic stress were not men soldiers but women civilians.

This spurred on the creation of sexual assault centers, the development of resources for survivors, and specific research into the alarmingly common trauma experienced by women. Initial focus was placed on rape, seen primarily as a random act of violence and assault committed by a stranger. But eventually, awareness grew around more private and pervasive types of sexual abuse in domestic settings.

Finally, the picture became clearer, and what it revealed was grim. Recent research indicates that one in every three girls and one in every seven boys will be victims of sexual abuse before they turn eighteen.[2] In approximately 80 percent of cases, the perpetrator is a family member, with nearly the entire remaining 20 percent of cases involving another known friend or acquaintance.[3] One out of every ten children lives in a home against which reports of abuse have been filed with protective service agencies,[4] a statistic made even more sobering by the reality that many cases of child sexual abuse go unreported. Global statistics indicate that nearly 20 percent of women worldwide have faced sexual abuse during childhood,[5] and domestic violence remains the number one reason that women in the US seek emergency medical care.[6]

Though it wasn't until late in the twentieth century that sexual trauma became normalized as a topic of study, researchers many decades before had in fact discovered clear connections between sexual abuse and the psychological disruption it causes. In the nineteenth century, scientists began studying a phenomenon they called "hysteria." For many years the term was used as a broad category for various psychological and emotional symptoms, generally believed to relate specifically to women and to be rooted in the uterus (thus the name "hysteria"). The women were perceived as devious and lazy, attempting to avoid serious work. But eventually they received the attention of famed neurologist Jean-Martin Charcot. His work helped in small ways to dignify these women by viewing their symptoms more objectively, without the skepticism and disdain of prior clinicians, albeit still in a detached fashion.

One of Charcot's most distinguished successors, Sigmund Freud, took up his mantle and furthered his research by entering more fully into the world of these "hysterical" women. Despite Charcot's insistence that sexuality was not related to his patients' ailments, Freud's studies quickly surfaced another truth. It became clear that psychological trauma was the root of hysteria.

As Freud spent significant time interviewing these women, he detected a clear and common pattern of sexual abuse. Freud also noted that when women were able to articulate their experiences, their symptoms decreased, a finding that spurred the development of the now widely regarded procedure of psychotherapy.[7] After hearing repeated accounts of women's abusive experiences, Freud published a still-renown paper entitled "The Aetoliogy of Hysteria," in which he contended the following: "I therefore put forward the thesis that at the bottom of every case of hysteria there are one or more occurrences of premature sexual experience, occurrences which belong to the earliest years of childhood."[8] This report was groundbreaking in its field. At long last, it appeared that these women might finally be believed, that their stories of trauma might be heard and honored.

But soon Freud began to reflect on the social implications of his theories. Given the pervasiveness of hysteria among women, Freud's hypothesis forced the conclusion that what he termed "perverted acts against children"[9] occurred with alarming frequency among all strata of society, in rich and poor households alike. For Freud to retain and further develop his initial theories that exposed the exploitation and traumatization of women, he would have had to ally himself with the budding feminist movement, a direct contradiction to his staunchly patriarchal commitments.

This proved too inconvenient a truth and too difficult a decision for Freud to manage. He soon rejected his earlier claims and reformulated his approach toward his women patients. In the face of personal unease and public critique, Freud vehemently repudiated his earlier findings, going so far as to claim that the women had made up their accounts of abuse. Freud and the sociopolitical context he inhabited were not yet willing to affirm this type of exploration into the inner worlds of the most traumatized, not yet willing to believe women.[10]

Near the turn of the twentieth century, after his final case study on hysteria with a young woman who experienced what would now be named as human sex trafficking, Freud leveled this devastating claim: "I was at last obliged to recognize that these scenes of seduction had never taken place, and that they were only fantasies which my patients had made up."[11] Freud began studying women's sexual experiences not as trauma and abuse but as sexualized fantasies and desires that they sought to enact. In other words, they were asking for it.

With the opportunity in his grasp to honor women's experiences, to call out every system of power that perpetuated these abuses, Freud instead labeled the women liars and blamed them for their pain. And we've been doing the same ever since.

When I think about introducing God language to interface with sexual trauma survivors' pain, I feel all sorts of hesitation. There are just so very many pitfalls and risks. Women's suffering has too often been glorified in religious circles, causing women to believe that there is a salvific quality to what they experience. Jesus willingly obeyed, after all. He took on the pain. You can endure in yours! And there will be a reward for you in doing so![12]

These absurdly harmful theologies arise in patriarchal contexts that force women into a subordinated status, praising such unjust hierarchies as God's intent. Women—and indeed, all of creation—will never be able to fully flourish within such walls.

So here we look to Jesus not as one forced to bear our punishments and endure the wrath of an angry God. Rather, we see Jesus as a force of love who embodied compassion and humility, a revolutionary who refused to employ violent or coercive tools to his ends. He rejected every dehumanizing system that valued power, profit, and prestige over life. He gave of himself willingly in service to the most marginalized. And like so many others who violate the norms established by the powers at hand, he ended up on a cross. Here, at the very site of his deepest pain, he eschewed patriarchal power that builds itself up through the exploitation of others. He embraced the full human condition, and he dignified it.

As one who suffered with us, Jesus believes our experiences of suffering. He believes the stories women tell about their abuse, because he experienced the very same in his own body. He was stripped naked. He was held down. He was bound. He was pierced. His flesh was torn and he bled. His naked, wounded, vulnerable body was put on display for others to view, while his abusers mocked him and gambled for his bloody underwear. All who saw Jesus's crucifixion knew who held the power and who would be forced to submit to it. His crucifixion was a public act of sexual violation.

Jesus's story is that of the billions of women and children around the world who are raped, assaulted, harassed, abused, trafficked, tortured, exploited, killed. The cross is God's great act of solidarity with humanity, joining us in the places of our deepest suffering and trauma and saying, "Me too."

The body of Christ endured sexual abuse, and the body of Christ still does. While survivors in churches and communities and societies may be silenced, may be blamed for their trauma, may be called liars and sluts, God believes them because she knows what it's like to suffer in her own body.

And like the survivors we are and the survivors we know, God received death and transformed it into life. The powers believed they got to pronounce the final word. They thought that if they silenced anyone who dare question their systems, they could keep hold of the reigns. Rather than agreeing to their terms and playing by the rules of their twisted game, Jesus took violence and abuse and—like turning water into wine—he transmuted them. He showed us what true power looks like. And he took back the narrative.

God has always been One Who Suffers *With*, one who willingly makes herself vulnerable to and with humanity. When our survival instincts tell us to withdraw and withhold, she extends herself. When despotic leaders accumulate power and lord it over others, she gives of herself. She speaks of another way and she embodies it.

To speak of God as One Who Suffers With does not explain away suffering itself. Anyone who has endured abuse, violence, or trauma would be right to question the order of things, to question God. I question too. I weep and wail at the world's absurd and overwhelming pains. I feel anger, rage even. I so want a world without such heinous suffering or at least a God who prevents it. And in the next breath I sense the felt need to somehow defend God and stick up for her, to offer clever theological rationale for the existence of evil and God's goodness still.

But just as the body is the crime scene for sexual abuse survivors, the body is where we must turn our focus. As my friend Richard Beck names, we tend to shift into our brains as we try to develop a theodicy, an explanation that vindicates God in the midst of the world's evils. But our response to suffering cannot be an intellectual one. "Our response to suffering isn't theological debate and mental rumination—a big pile of questions, doubts, and existential breakdowns. . . . Our response must be *action*. Resistance is our only theodicy."[13]

We bear the image of God. And she bears the very same wounds we do. So let us run toward every corner of suffering and speak words of healing. Let us dismantle every vestige of power that perpetuates abuse and silences victims and build a better world for everyone.[14] Let us believe the stories of survivors and together live into better narratives where we are the subject and never an object. And let us name our traumas and reveal our scars alongside the God who does the same.

God Is Wisdom Within

Everything in the universe is within you.

—Rumi

The truth is, we do know and we know that we know.

—Julia Cameron

you will greet yourself arriving
at your own door, in your own mirror,
. . .
and say, sit here. Eat.
You will love again the stranger who was your self.

— "Love After Love," Derek Walcott

Before becoming a parent, I imagined that kids come into the world like empty vessels. It was the parents' job to fill them with all sorts of knowledge and truth and wisdom, to teach them all they need to know and make sure they eat their vegetables.

Then I became a parent. And I realized that those babies come into the world already who they are, and that my primary job—especially for the first several years—is to keep them alive so they can express just that.

This has never felt like a devaluation of my role as a parent, just a beautiful recalibration of it. There's plenty we teach children in our care, and I'll always be worried about how much of the kale on their plates they've eaten. But I've realized just how deeply connected tiny humans are to innate wisdom, to their true self, and it's helped me connect with my own.

When my girls were infants, I spent an inordinate amount of time getting them to sleep. I'd bounce and I'd sway and I'd sing and I'd pat and I'd just about drive myself mad trying to convince these babies to close their eyes and sleep. I was exhausted and they were too, and I knew that if we all could just get some rest then maybe we could survive the day. When at long last they would succumb to the movement and fall asleep, my first move was not to my own bed or the couch. Most often, I would sit in the nursery chair and just keep holding them.

It was counterintuitive. It didn't make sense. All I wanted was for them to sleep and finally they were doing just that, yet there I stayed. I didn't fully understand it at the time—I don't *fully* understand it now—but there was some sort of energy they exuded that I just wanted to be in the presence of. I wanted to feel, to hold, to take in. I still do.

An indigenous teaching holds that babies come into the world knowing everything they need to know. Soon, the trauma and chaos of the world cause them to forget it, so they spend their lives relearning what they already knew, waking up to what they've always known.

This is why I would linger in the girls' nursery. I could sense that they knew much more than they could say, that their memory contained multitudes, that when they lay their heads on my chest I somehow got access to a mystery I too once knew. A mystery I wanted to know again.

The world's religions and traditions, philosophies and spiritualities reflect truth and beauty in various and sometimes conflicting ways. But a thread that ties each of them together is the consistent theme of awareness, this insistence on waking up to your self and paying attention. Many call this consciousness, the you behind the you. Practitioners of meditation spend their lives cultivating this full awareness, but infants are *masters* of it.

There are four kinds of brainwaves, the signals that our brains use to communicate with our bodies as they organize and process the various stimuli they perceive. Scans reveal that newborns and infants most often produce delta brain waves, the slowest of the four. They're associated with a sense of peacefulness and relaxation, with restorative rest and regeneration. Adults in deep sleep or in calm, meditative states produce these slow brain waves. Most often, though, adults produce beta waves, which are the quickest and most chaotic. In moderation they are essential, but a chronic state of beta waves reflects high levels of anxiety, obsessiveness, and restlessness.

We come into the world at peace, brimming with Divine Wisdom and awake to ourselves. But for most of us, it doesn't take long for our journeys to quickly alter course. The chaos of our world, the dysfunction of our homes, the vulnerabilities of life shift us away from the modes of being and knowing we were born with. They propel us into frenzied, frenetic energies, and we become disconnected from our own selves.

Over the last several years, I've been on an exploration to rediscover my truest self, a journey back to myself. And I've encountered God at each step. I grew up in a tradition that emphasized seeking out God's wisdom in making decisions. I was encouraged to pray and to listen. I wasn't given much in the way of how to discern God's voice or make sense of what I heard (or didn't hear), but I learned enough to believe that God was close to us and I could connect with God.

This was far more than some of my friends received. Their traditions placed clear and secure limits around the times in history when God spoke and times in history—including now—when God decided to shut up. The only place where you could get a sense of God's voice was in the biblical texts, which were of course explained by men preachers and scholars who made absolutely certain claims about what God meant. Apparently they could keep talking, but God had given it up a long time ago.

Chapter 12

For all of its faults, my faith tradition offered a more generous understanding. Some of the most profound moments of my early spirituality were times I prayed, seeking wisdom and guidance, and I heard God speak in reply. It was never a loud or overwhelming voice, just a gentle but unmistakable clarity in my spirit. Years and even decades later, I still hold these encounters dear.

But then I got older. I came face to face with some of the wounded places within me that needed healing, and I sought out the companions I needed for that journey—a therapist and a spiritual director. My work with each took slightly different forms, each with its own focus and particulars. But rising to the surface of it all has been the continuous thread of coming home to myself. And in this work, I began to hear my *own* voice.

Sitting with my therapist, I would ramble on about what I was thinking and wondering about and trying to make sense of. I would shift into the part of my left brain that humans use to make meaning of our experiences, where we rationalize and analyze and work for it all to make sense. These are essential processes, but it's easy to get stuck there. We can try to make meaning of an experience that we are, in fact, refusing to actually *experience*.

So my therapist would invite me to connect with myself. To check in with my body to feel what it was holding and where. To make note of any emotions that surfaced and what they felt like. To notice if I was trying to tell myself any messages. And every single time, I was. She would ask if the source of the voice I was hearing was internal or external, and every time I could only say "yes." It was emanating from within me and required my consciousness, but it was also bigger and more and beyond me.

I would hear affirmations of who I am and what I'm capable of. Reminders about the world and its abundance. Insight into how I could move forward in life-giving ways. It was beautiful, clarifying, full. But almost without fail, I would soon hear other voices whose words were not as affirming. I know that triggers alarm bells for some who might immediately want to call a psychiatrist or an exorcist, but either option would be to miss what was actually going on for me.

My faith tradition confidently labeled any voice perceived as negative to be demonic, evil, dark.[1] I was taught (and by many still encouraged) to pray against the devil, to resist what he was telling me with confident truths about God. "That's just the enemy talking," they would say. "He loves to attack us when we're weak." I'm not as interested in evaluating here the particulars of this worldview on a broad scale[2] as I am interested in saying this: to label as evil every voice we hear that isn't uttering kind or encouraging words is to bypass a treasure trove of meaning-laden messages we're trying to send ourselves, messages that can lead to profound awareness and deep healing.

When I take time to thoughtfully check in with myself, it doesn't take long for parts of me to begin responding from fear and shame. Wisdom Within tells me that I am enough, that I can resist the felt need to perform and please. She helps me see that when I walk into a space, my default response is to continually scan the room, seeking to determine how I'm being perceived by others. She ignites my imagination to see a different way of entering that space, one where I walk in a full sense of self and I'm not tethered to others' assessments. It's beautiful and compelling and just as soon as I believe it's true, other parts of me begin to speak otherwise.

"You can't be serious. Don't delude yourself into thinking that's possible. You know they only love you for what you do and how well you can do it. Are you seriously thinking of putting your ideas out there? That is *way* too vulnerable. Did you see how they reacted when you said what you thought? How could you be so stupid. You'll never be enough. Just stay small and be quiet."

These voices have real effect, and their arguments are compelling. But when I take the time to fully hear them out, neither evaluating nor diminishing them, I realize that behind the megaphone stand wounded, scared parts of myself trembling in fear. Parts that wallow in shame and can only offer sentiments dripping with it. I realize that these voices are trying to protect me, to keep me safe. They don't want to hurt me. They're trying to prevent me *from* being hurt.

Suddenly, instead of silencing them or suppressing them or praying them away, I'm able to hold deep, resounding compassion for them. For *me*. I'm able to extend kindness to them the same way I would if I saw a scared, trembling five-year-old—because in fact, that is exactly what's happening.

Our earliest traumas cause us to splinter ourselves into parts in order to survive.[3] Some parts carry the pain into exile, staying below the surface and out of our consciousness. Some parts act out in obsessive or compulsive ways, reacting to what we've experienced and numbing out when the pain resurfaces. Some parts rise up to manage all the others, keeping them in check and remaining on high alert for any potential new traumas.

When I go inward and listen to the many voices, I realize how long these parts of me have been at work to protect me, how much energy they've exerted seeking to stay safe, how utterly exhausted they are. Flooded with empathy and compassion, I embrace them. My truest self sees and names and honors them. I thank them for the countless ways they've worked to help me interface with the world and survive in it. And then, I release them from their duty. Feet firmly rooted in my fullest, truest self, I hold their hands and let them know that they are free, that they can rest. I show them the woman they've helped me become. I assure them that I have every resource needed within to step fully into my life. And I remind them about the Wisdom Within that always has been mine, the voice they once knew and trusted and can learn to know and trust once more.

In the Bible, Wisdom is not simply a desired attribute or virtue. Wisdom is a person. She is fierce and loud and brave and strong. She walks through the streets with confidence and purpose. She knows what she knows; she is who she is. And she calls out to anyone willing to listen, using her voice to proclaim truth and beauty so that everyone might benefit from her.

In a stunning passage in Proverbs 8, we learn how she came to be and what she roots herself in.

> YHWH gave birth to me at the beginning,
> before the first acts of creation.
> I have been from everlasting,
> in the beginning, before the world began.
> Before the deep seas, I was brought forth,
> before there were fountains or springs of water;
> before the mountains erupted up into place,
> before the hills, I was born—
> before God created the earth or its fields,
> or even the first clods of dirt.
> I was there when the Almighty created the heavens,
> and set the horizon just above the ocean,
> set the clouds in the sky,
> and established the springs of the deep,
> gave the seas their boundaries
> and set the limits at their shoreline.
> When the foundation of the earth was laid out,
> I was the skilled artisan standing next to the Almighty.
> I was God's delight day after day,
> rejoicing at being in God's presence continually,
> rejoicing in the whole world
> and delighting in humankind.
>
> (Prov. 8:22–31, Inclusive Bible)

Of course she's such a badass! She's been around since the beginning of all things, the "skilled artisan" beside the Creator calling the universe into being. If cultural or societal or religious forces dare tried to keep her quiet and small, she'd remind them that she has "been from everlasting" and that their contextual and time-bound particulars will fall as quickly as they came about. But Wisdom? Like the mountains whose birth she attended, she will endure.

We're told that she speaks at the city center where everyone can hear her—not in exclusive boardrooms or to segregated groups, but right in the middle of everyone. She speaks with authority and without apology. She knows what she knows and she brings it into speech. She exudes the kind of true, abiding confidence that emanates regality without a hint of pride or condescension. She is available to all—without exception—because her ways are just. And her ways *lead* to justice (Prov. 8:20).

God has never been stingy with God's self. Rather, God is willing to inhabit human form (John 1:14) and reside within bodies (1 Cor. 6:19). Wisdom has been *ours* from the very beginning. But for myriad reasons, we too often live without any awareness of her.

Women are especially conditioned to forget about the Wisdom Within. While pursuing her Master of Divinity, a friend of mine focused her research on people's self-perception of their gifts. She wanted to know how they understood their own gifts and abilities, and whether they felt welcome or able to use these gifts in their faith community. In large numbers, men identified themselves as exceling in leadership and teaching, confident in claiming authority and speaking from it. But the women identified themselves as good listeners, ones who are able to encourage others, to give care, to love.

God knows the world needs more good listeners, but I so desperately want women to know that they are worth being listened *to*. I want every human being to know that we possess Wisdom Within, a connection to the Divine that goes back to the first-ever moment that was, carried in our ancestors through every season, and somehow just as full and immediate and present within us now.

I know our faith traditions tell us otherwise. They tell us that all authority is external, to be found only in texts and scholars and traditions. They fear what it may mean for God really to have unleashed herself within every human being across the planet, and they teach us to fear the same. But Wisdom Within is ours.

I know that our traumas tell us otherwise. They tell us we can't trust ourselves, that we didn't foresee the abuse or the loss and couldn't tell someone what we needed. They tell us that we don't get a say in what happens in our lives and that even if we did, we would just mess the whole thing up anyway. Our traumas rob us of our voice and keep us silent. But Wisdom Within is ours.

I know our cultures tell us otherwise. They tell us to listen to the best marketing campaigns and advertising slogans, to let others decide what is good for us. They structure humans by race and class and sex and ability and dole out only so much authority to a select few in what they tell us is a zero-sum game. But Wisdom Within is *ours*.

This innate wisdom is a powerful coalescence of Divine Source and our individual, unique, beautiful personhood. It is both within us and beyond us. It is ours and it is everyone's. It is old and new, perennial and fresh. It is our birth right as human beings made in the image of God. And it requires our participation, our willingness to believe that we really are capable of possessing Wisdom Within and listening to it.

I am under no delusions that I am God. But when I pray, when I take time to listen, I hear a Voice that grounds me, guides me, moves me, compels me, roots me. It is not the voice of my ego or my trauma or any part of me bent on self-protection. It draws from a much deeper well.

In those encounters I cannot clearly distinguish between my own voice and that of God and frankly, I've lost interest in trying to. Because I've come to see that my truest self is so open to Wisdom Within that, like a newborn lying perfectly at peace on her mama's chest, she remembers the stuff she's made of.

13

God Is Home

We may act sophisticated and worldly but I believe we feel safest when we go inside ourselves and find home, a place where we belong and maybe the only place we really do.

—Maya Angelou

I arise in the morning torn between a desire to improve the world and a desire to enjoy the world. This makes it hard to plan the day.

—E. B. White

We know that from the beginning until now, all of creation has been groaning in one great act of giving birth. And not only creation, but all of us who possess the firstfruits of the Spirit—we too groan inwardly as we wait for our bodies to be set free.

—Romans 8:22–23 (Inclusive Bible)

As best as I can recall, I first encountered the Spirit Who Groans Within when I was five or six. I wouldn't have called it that at the time. It was only later in life, having repeated experiences, that I began to find language for the burdens I felt at such a young age.

I didn't have the language then. All I knew was that my heart felt like it weighed a hundred pounds, a condition my friends didn't seem to suffer from. They seemed to function like normal kids, relatively carefree and at ease, unhindered by the weight I was always carrying. I read *The Diary of Anne Frank* as soon as I learned to read. I watched Holocaust documentaries and read books about concentration camp survivors. I was drawn to anything that was broken, anything that was dark and, frankly, anything that was depressing.

One night I was invited to a neighbor's sixth birthday party. I showed up late because I couldn't be dragged away from the TV special I was watching. It detailed all of the maniacal ways the Nazis developed to exterminate the Jews and anyone deemed "other." When I finally made my way to the party, sick to my stomach and sad as hell, I was horrified.

Here was a house full of hyper kids, wearing gaudy party hats and stuffing their faces with cupcakes, running around like a bunch of idiots who didn't seem to know or understand the horrors of our world. Had these kids not seen the black and white footage of starving men and women being pushed into pits that would become their unmarked mass grave? They hadn't. Did they not care that humanity could be so cruel and inflict such suffering on its own kind? They didn't. Needless to say, I didn't stick around for cake.

It's silly to think about it now, but it has never felt silly. It has felt like a constant weight I've had no choice but to carry. I began groaning under the weight as a small child, and I've been groaning ever since.

To be sure, I had a beautiful childhood. My life has seen no shortage of gifts and beauty and love, moments where my response is one of deep joy and gratitude: bottles of wine and vulnerable conversations shared with friends who know how to hold your soul with care; the so-deep-its-painful love I feel when I look at my daughters and strain to understand how I had any part in their coming to be; the way the sun infuses my bones with warmth and clouds move like sky dancers in creative expression; sensing the risk of being fully known by my husband and being met with his daily commitment to partner in this life together; chances to bring my gifts to bear in ways that serve the world and fill my soul. These are moments where I want to stop and set up an altar in the world and say this is *good*. This is God.

And then there are moments where I glimpse a photo of the limp body of a three-year-old refugee, lying lifeless on the sand of a shoreline that was supposed to mean freedom. My fingertips can still recall the sensation of holding my three-year-old nephew as he fell asleep on my chest the night before I saw that photo. And all I can do is weep and wail and groan for the disparities, for the ways death insists on rearing its head again and again and again.

I watch footage of yet another Black man murdered in the street by a police officer in a modern-day lynching, and I groan.

I see migrant children held in cages at the border, stripped from their parents and anything that would signal safety, and I groan.

I read statistics of how many trans women have been murdered or gone missing this year, and I groan.

I sit across from another woman as she shares about the violation of her body and dignity through sexual assault, a story her church refused to believe and instead asked that she remain silent, and I groan.

I hear the story of a White supremacist, loaded with weapons and filled with hatred, opening fire on Muslim worshippers in their holy place, and I groan.

I feel the same way I felt as a six-year-old watching footage of mothers being ripped apart from their children and men stripped of their dignity and masses of humans marched to their death like cattle to a slaughterhouse. My body aches and my heart sinks and I scream out, "It was never meant to be like this! There has to be another way!" And somewhere along the way my pleas turn to cries. My cries turn to sounds. And my sounds turn to groans. Evolutionary processes reverse and I lose my capacities for intellect and articulation and I simply utter sounds too deep and weighty for words.

But then I listen. And I begin to notice that the sounds I utter are vibrating at the same frequency as the sounds of creation, their rhythms and patterns and noises echoed by the mountains and the trees and the oceans and the land.

These pillars of creation, themselves spoken into existence by beautiful and life-giving words, are capable of uttering only sounds. Their groans convey a wild and deep despair for what creation witnesses: the soil that soaks up innocent blood which seems to run like a river; the waves that carry the drowning bodies of families desperate to seek refuge from war and destruction; the trees and habitat that are pillaged by humans fueled only by greed and the consuming desire for more; the mountains that forge the dangerous path to higher ground for men and women and children hoping to find passage into the sky and away from the chaos.

Creation sees and feels and knows the weight. It joins the chorus of those who know no other response but to groan for the world that is not yet as it should be. I have never struggled to groan for the world's suffering. What *is* a challenge, however, is knowing what to do with my own suffering.

Next to the stories of so many others, I feel no right to claim hardship or pain. Any difficulties I may face or grief I may feel simply pales in comparison. To claim my own "trauma" when the world endures traumas I never could imagine? No, I'll just keep that one to myself.

I've become something of an expert at diminishing what I feel. Sure, I may be exhausted by the daily demands of parenting, but I have access to resources so I really should be okay. I may sense anger about being silenced within patriarchal structures, but I'm a White privileged woman so who am I to complain. I may feel anxiety about an overwhelming number of tasks and responsibilities, but I have a stable job and income so there's no room for self-pity here. I may be mourning the loss of someone close to me, but surely others have known far more death and are more deserving of this meal from a friend than I am. I may have been harmed by seeing sexually explicit images at a very young age, which is technically considered a form of sexual abuse, but I wasn't abused like the women around me so it's not as big of a deal.

Whatever my experience, whatever my pain, it will never match that of others, so it just doesn't get to be as real. There's no time to honor what I feel when there's even greater suffering in the world. Creation is groaning for *them*, but surely not for me.

This pattern is so ingrained that even as I write about it here, a little voice inside tells me I've assessed things properly: *What's there to critique? Why take up this space for yourself?* But hours of self-reflection and meditation and years of therapy and spiritual direction force me to pause, to bring this dynamic into my conscious awareness, and to hold it with curiosity. In doing so, I've come to realize that I developed this pattern through the merging of three seemingly disparate but wildly powerful forces: my internal shame management system, bad theology, and colonialism.

From age five, I recognized that in order to keep shame at bay and to present as the good little girl I wanted to be perceived as, I needed to perform. I needed to succeed, to accomplish, to achieve. This kind of laser-like focus requires enormous time and energy. Feelings? They're a hindrance. They get in the way. They complicate life and inhibit me from getting things done.

I have an uncanny ability to spot a feeling coming down the pipeline, pull it off the conveyor belt, and set it on a shelf before it has time to reach me. There's no time for sadness or fear when tasks need to be done. And so we press on. This kind of suppression works really well, until it doesn't.

Our emotions are meant to be experienced, felt, *honored*, not stifled. So from an early age, mine just came out sideways. What I could not feel for myself, I felt for others a thousand times over. I doubled down on holding compassion for everyone else, all the while refusing to offer any to the scared little girl within.

I wish my faith tradition had offered me a better story here, but truthfully it just reinforced these harmful internal systems. I heard no shortage of sermons affirming that I was, in fact, bad and sinful. I remember hearing one minister talk about how we were like "filthy rags" to God (drawn from a text in Isaiah 64), and compare those filthy rags to women's sanitary napkins. This confirmed two things to me: I was dirty, bad, wrong, and women were especially so. But thankfully there was a masculine God who could save me from myself, and maybe even from my womanhood too.

It's quite a leap from that kind of theology to honoring one's own experiences and feelings. It makes much more sense to suppress your emotions, or worse, to blame yourself for feeling them.

My personal shame management system developed within the context of this faith system, which developed within the context of Western colonialism. Here, every impulse is toward doing, conquering, controlling, mastering, subduing. Here, productivity, overwork, and exhaustion are considered virtues, signs of one's worth and value. You cannot extend an empire's reach by taking naps and meditating; you gotta get to work. Every aspect of toxic masculinity is on display here, with the constant felt need to push and force and coerce. There is no time to check in with yourself, to practice selfcare, to take a break. You're feeling sad or scared or confused or lonely? Suck it up, soldier. There's work to be done.

This can all get *really* confusing when the work you're trying to do is intended to serve the world, not conquer it.

For so many of us, we've been groaning about various forms of injustice and trying to put our hands to work in meaningful ways, but these colonial impulses still surge within. Sure, maybe I'm not striving to become a billionaire and spend my profits to play in space. Maybe I'm not a politician rubbing shoulders with interest groups, intent on winning at all costs. But I'm no less capable of pushing myself to the extreme in service of a just cause, all the while causing inestimable harm to my own soul.

To move forward in a different way, we need a vision for what it could look like. We need our imaginations to be stirred toward creative possibilities.

The Hebrew Scriptures provide for me one such vision. After rescuing the Israelites from horrifying enslavement in Egypt, God gives them a series of commands to order their new communal life. Before and during and after the commands are pronounced, God says, "Remember when you were slaves in Egypt." It's this continued refrain that reminds them of the oppression they had endured, lest they ever forget it. But it's also a call to build their new community in a way that wouldn't keep such injustice in cycle, so they couldn't shift from oppressed to oppressor.

It's a series of imperfect laws that were never carried out completely, but the vision it casts of a new kind of world is stunning. There are commands about how, when you're gleaning your field, not to push to the edges but rather always to leave crops in place so that foreigners, orphans, and widows could take from the harvest. There are commands limiting the amount of time someone could indenture themselves to work for you in order to pay back a debt so that systemic poverty wouldn't have a chance to develop. There are commands about regular and consistent rest, ensuring that not only the human laborers but the animals and land itself would get a break. All of these and more point to a way of ordering life such that everyone and everything has the capacity to *flourish*.

It's in these texts that I begin to imagine another way of being, one that allows for me to groan for the world's suffering but also to groan for my own. A world where there is space enough for the tears of my neighbors and the tears I cry for myself. A rhythm of good, meaningful work to enact justice in the world, and good, holy rest for my body and spirit.

I long for this way of being, and the only place I've ever really experienced it is at Home.

Home is the space where I get to be seen, to be known, to matter. Where I may leave a thousand times but I'm received with open arms upon every return. Where I glimpse what it might mean to be a human *being* instead of a human *doing*.

When I was eighteen, I moved away from home for college and, as my dad is fond of lamenting, "never came back." I hadn't intended this. I had lived my whole life in the same zip code, same city, same house, with all of my extended family living within fifteen miles of each other. I grew up five minutes from the beach and spent endless hours there, knowing full well that I lived in paradise. Every family has its dysfunctions and mine has never been immune, but all the same, home remains for me the safest place I know.

I can close my eyes and in an instant, I'm on the beach digging my toes in the sand and feeling the waves on my skin, sensing my cells vibrate at a frequency they only do when I'm grounded in the stuff I'm made of. I'm in my grandmother's house with cousins running around and playing games, our family sharing Sunday lunch and arguing about politics and yelling at the football referees on TV. I'm on the back deck of the house I grew up in, sitting in the sunshine and soaking it in like it may one day run out.

Home is where I belong, where I get to receive. It's where my mama nursed me, where my grandmothers rocked me, where my aunts baked me birthday cakes, where my family fed me. Home is where I get to receive these gifts—not because I've performed well enough, and not because the world's sufferings finally have ceased. I get to receive simply because I am worthy of receiving.

I have a home of my own now, a space where my girls will make their memories and grow into who they are. And here, I get to choose my way of being. I can choose to deny my own experience and suppress my feelings and diminish my pain, to run myself ragged and work myself into a breakdown claiming that I'm just trying to take care of the world. Or, I can choose instead to resist injustice with joy, to believe that every decision I make says yes to a certain version of the world, even the choice to honor my feelings and take that bubble bath.

I don't know how to choose this way unless God is Home. If God is not the very space in which I am free to be a human who cares for the world and to receive the very same care, the space in which I can groan for the pain of others and be comforted in my own pain, then I am left with no other option but to *be* God. I must bear the world's burdens and right all of its wrongs. I must focus on everyone else and never myself. I must keep pushing harder and going further in a relentless pursuit to hold the whole world in my hands. But the memories of my home tell me another way is possible. The home I'm now creating for my own family helps me live into this new way. The God I come to understand more fully in these spaces affirms it.

Once when Olive was quite small, we were walking through a store in midsummer. The fall décor was already on display, likely put out the moment the Valentine's candy was gone. As my husband Tim and I talked, Olive pointed to the round, orange object on the shelf and said "pumpkin." We had never taught her this word or heard her say it before, and like any obnoxious parent who knows their kid is the smartest in the world, we laughed at how brilliant she was.

Somewhat tongue in cheek, I knelt next to her and asked, "Olive, what is God like?" She paused only for a moment.

"Home," she said.

I'm trying to live my life believing that she was exactly right.

God Is Mystery

All saying must be balanced by unsaying, and knowing must be humbled by unknowing. Without this balance, religion invariably becomes arrogant, exclusionary, and even violent.

—Richard Rohr

I want to ask you, as clearly as I can, to bear with patience all that is unresolved in your heart, and try to love the questions themselves.... For everything must be lived. Live the questions now, perhaps then, someday, you will gradually, without noticing, live into the answer.

—Rainer Marie Rilke, "Letter to a Young Poet"

Silence is the language of God. All else is poor translation.

—Rumi

I have two recurring nightmares. In the first, I find myself in high school on the last day of the school year, when suddenly I realize there was a class I was supposed to have attended all year but somehow forgot about. Now, in the final minutes of the semester, I have no possible way to make up this work, and I am left standing in a hallway full of bustling summer-ready teens, utterly dumbfounded at my mistake. In the second nightmare, I am going about my day when suddenly I recall a flight that I need to take and it leaves in thirty minutes, leaving me about thirty *seconds* to pack a suitcase in which I will undoubtedly forget essential items and not have what I need on said trip. (*Is anyone else starting to sweat?*)

Someone with greater training might be able to analyze these dreams with precision, but knowing enough about myself and the absurdities of my subconscious, here is what these nightmares point to: I am terrified of not having control. I don't like being caught off guard. Control requires great preparation, and the thought of having neglected this essential preparation is, quite literally, a nightmare.

I don't know to what extent this reflects normal, evolutionary impulses shared by all human beings, but I do know that maintaining control has long been a means of survival for me. From my earliest experiences of shame, I knew I would need to function in a perfectly controlled way so that no one would have the chance to see the bad little girl I was. This requires enormous focus and preparation, such that something like a hastily packed suitcase could threaten the whole system. If I'm caught off guard without my toothbrush or proper shoes, if I could be so foolish as to forget about a course or an assignment, then suddenly I am vulnerable and the weaknesses in my shame management system—the weaknesses in *me*—are exposed.

I'm convinced that what is true at this micro level is also true at a systemic level. Vulnerability does not build empires; control does. Tribal identities demand clear distinctions between who is and who is not a member of the community, who is in and who is out. Political parties do not win elections by humanizing everyone and occupying complexity; entire campaigns are built around unmistakable assertions of their rightness and the other party's wrongness. Religious institutions don't gain dominance through a generous orthodoxy; they do so through exclusionary statements of faith that define—and demand—right thinking.

Sitting in a space of uncertainty, of complexity, of mystery is *hard*. So in big and small ways, we cling to what feels certain and stable, believing this to be a more secure option.

My brother is a successful attorney in Tampa, which gives me what feels like a superpower access to court proceedings and the legal system. I love to pick his brain about cases, crafting my own closing arguments in my head as I do, certain I would woo a jury in my client's favor.

Recently my brother shared with me about his process of securing an expert witness for a medical malpractice case he was overseeing. Expert witnesses in relevant fields are often summoned by law firms to offer their opinions on a matter. They speak to whether what happened in a case was, according to their training and experience, proper or not. These experts can be a helpful external voice in what is oftentimes a complicated case presented to a jury.

My brother mentioned that in virtually all cases he's worked, the jury sides with the expert witness's opinion. I began to wonder about this. What is it about hearing from a so-called expert that makes one more inclined to believe them? I wondered about the emotional weight of rejecting an expert witness's opinion. To have someone held out as an "expert" and decide that perhaps they are wrong in their assessment feels like pulling a loose brick out of a wall, only to wonder what other bricks might be poorly constructed, only to realize that if this wall comes down, I'll be buried underneath it.

If this expert is questionable, what might that say about the system (legal, educational, medical, religious, etc.) they represent? What might that say about the truths on which I've constructed my reality and made sense of the world? And am I being misled? These are big questions, *hard* questions. They might not be in the forefront of a juror's mind as she listens to testimony in a case, but I have to wonder if these questions aren't at least firing in the subconscious.

My point is not to evaluate the validity of expert witness testimony—I'll leave that to actual lawyers instead of aspiring closing argument writers—but rather to name the ways that the human desire for certainty and security are very real, with very real impact.

In Aldous Huxley's *Brave New World*, a utopian society—the "World State"—has been formed through genetic engineering and social conditioning to maximize social happiness: a singular, utilitarian pursuit that requires rejection of art, of individuality, of emotion, of nature, of love. The World State's motto is "Community, Identity, Stability." The story's protagonist, John (also called "The Savage"), experiences life in this highly engineered world and decides he wants to return to his native land, a world not yet touched by the World State. Mustapha Mond, one of the World State's supreme leaders, tries to reason with John, reminding him of the comforts secured through this structured system, the guarantees of perpetual happiness. John resists:

> "But I don't want comfort. I want God, I want poetry, I want real danger, I want freedom, I want goodness. I want sin."
>
> "In fact," says Mustapha Mond, "you're claiming the right to be unhappy."
>
> "All right then," said the Savage defiantly. "I'm claiming the right to be unhappy."
>
> "Not to mention the right to grow old and ugly and impotent; the right to have syphilis and cancer; the right to have too little to eat; the right to be lousy; the right to live in constant apprehension of what may happen tomorrow; the right to catch typhoid; the right to be tortured by unspeakable pains of every kind." There was a long silence.
>
> "I claim them all," said the Savage at last.[1]

"Good for you, John!" I think, cheering him on. "You're doing it right! You're willing to reject the false certainties hawked to you like cheap wares at a flea market and instead embrace the vulnerability and complexity of life! Inspiring, truly. Now if you'll excuse me I have a suitcase that needs to be triple checked."

These kinds of controlling, limiting impulses show up in our nightmares, our subconscious seeking to make sense of all the ways we feel unsafe in the world. They show up in the world's systems and structures, seeking to exert control and secure power. And they show up in our theologies, the ways we understand and name God.

Some cultures and traditions have always been more comfortable with mystery, allowing for and celebrating the Unknown, but the modern Western world built a system of rationalism and logic to snuff out that kind of fanciful, prescientific, magical thinking. It's as if your two options are to believe in a world of unicorns and mermaids or to take God seriously by insisting with certainty what God is like.

If that were possible, if we could engage the world and the Divine with utter certainty, ensuring that we were safe and that vulnerabilities and unknowns were eliminated, most of us would take that world. But it's not the world we've been given. It's not the *God* we've been given. Every time we think we fully know and understand the Divine, God twirls around and takes another form and invites us to dance with the Mystery, and shit if I didn't forget to pack proper dancing shoes.

When I sit with folks in spiritual direction sessions, I work to create a space wherein they can engage the Divine in new ways. Sometimes I'll lead them through a practice where they connect with God and themselves and sacred texts, but where they can only express what they notice in colors, images, or sensations. We remove the option of language so they can move into different spaces in their brain and spirit, spaces where the Mysterious Divine is waiting to be found.

Occasionally after the exercise they'll try to articulate what happened, they'll try to explain what they sensed. But the moment they seek to wrap language around the ineffable, it's as if the encounter is made of air and begins to dissipate. You can study air and make truthful claims about it but ultimately, air is made to be *inhaled*.

The Hebrew Scriptures record a famed encounter between Moses and the Divine (see Exod. 3). Having fled Egypt and the life he knew, having left behind all of the certainties and comforts of the pharaoh's palace, he finds himself smack in the middle of the desert herding sheep. Suddenly, something catches his eye: a bush aflame with fire but not consumed by it.

Approaching it, he hears a voice telling him to remove his sandals for the ground on which he stands is holy. He complies (because you don't have to fully understand something to know it's full of Divine energy). The voice begins to tell Moses about how he will emerge as a leader for the people of Israel, guiding them out of their slavery and oppression and into wide-open spaces where they will flourish.

Moses imagines himself recounting this story to people, certain they will think he's lost his mind and wondering if perhaps he has. He asks for a name. "Who should I say sent me?" Moses leans *into* his curiosity, his sense of wonder. When he sensed Holiness, he did not bow down and bow out of any real further engagement. He knows there's more going on than he can understand or make sense of, so he presses into it. And the name he's given is as mysterious as the encounter itself (3:14): "I AM who I AM."

"I will be what I will be."

"I will be who I will be."

"I will be who I am."

"I am who I will be."

Scholars and translators have wrestled with this text perhaps more than any other from the Hebrew Scriptures, which only highlights the reality that the answer Moses receives is not an end, not clarity, not certainty or the wrapping up of all loose pieces. It doesn't conclude the conversation. The name that God gives throws doors wide open into Greater Mystery with an invitation to explore it.

Most modern translations show the name as "Yahweh." But for many Jews, the name is considered unspeakable, unwritable even. To claim that one can speak of God with any certainty is to take God's name in vain—which God had something to say about (see Exod. 20:7).

Some have suggested that ultimately the name was not intended to be said or written but *breathed.* The four Hebrew letters that comprise the name—transliterated as YHWH—mean "to be." In Hebrew, this would sound something like *yod, he, vav, he*—in other words, it would sound like *breathing.* The letters mimic the sounds of inhaling and exhaling, the most basic and essential practice shared by every human across the planet, "our first and last word as we enter and leave this world."[2]

Moses's encounter happened right in the middle of nowhere, near a mountain whose name means "wasteland." Away from religious structures, away from temples, away from clear signs designating the place as holy. Sometimes I wonder what would have happened if instead the bush burned in the middle of the city or near a temple or inside a church, where it could be observed by political leaders or legal scholars or religious teachers. I wonder how quickly they may have set out to downplay what happened, to contain the potential ramifications, to explain it in three easy sermon points, to demystify it. I wonder how quickly I would have moved to do the same.

As I write this, I'm on week three of a hospital stay with my youngest daughter, Ivy. A viral infection led to numerous and terrifying complications in her lungs, each one compounding the other, forcing her little body to fight in order to live. She's had three surgeries in as many weeks, each one more invasive and painful.

I've talked with more doctors and nurses and technicians and care providers than I can count, each working to bring their various forms of expertise to bear in saving Ivy's life. In these spaces, I want certainty. I want to know that the surgeon has practiced for thirty-five years and is renowned in her field. I want to know that the nurse is checking off every task each time he enters the room, monitoring each and every change in Ivy's condition. I want to know that she will be okay, that she will heal and recover, that she will come home and live her life fully as she should.

There are real, concrete variables that can be monitored and measured. Care teams can assess her vitals and her progress and make decisions accordingly. But at the end of the day, even with every advance in medicine at their disposal and their collective decades of experience, no guarantee exists here.

I ask the doctor, "Am I foolish to believe that Ivy will get better, that she'll make it through this?" I hold back tears because I know she can't answer this question and I don't want to burden her with it.

But I have to name it. I have to articulate my desperation and fear and hopefulness. I seek a certain answer when I know there is none.

A few nights ago, Ivy developed another pneumothorax, causing a team of doctors to rush to her room and assess the situation. To have your child's bed surrounded by ten healthcare providers is equal parts encouraging that she is being cared for and utterly traumatizing knowing this level of care is required. Hours later, when the issue resolved and Ivy and I were alone in the hospital room that has become home, I lay with her on her bed coaxing her to sleep. I gently rubbed her face and softly sang the songs I've sung every night since she was born. I prayed and cried and felt a depth of exhaustion I never knew possible. After a while, I looked at her face and saw her eyes wide open, with a soft smirk on her lips. I smiled at her and she smiled at me.

"Ivy, do you remember God?"

Nod.

"Is she holding you now?"

Nod.

"And she's holding me now too."

Nod.

I wanted so badly to know if Ivy would be okay, if she would survive this fight and come home, if she could survive a pandemic with a disease that attacks the lungs—the very site of her sickness. I knew she couldn't tell me any of this. No one could. But as we lay there, no certainty or control to be found, I felt her trace my bracelet with her fingertips: a silver medallion on cream colored string with the words "open" and "expand" engraved on it.

On New Year's Eve, I chose these words as a symbol of the invitation I sensed being held out before me this year. I've been in a beautiful and difficult season of opening and expanding—myself, my world, my sense of the Divine. But on this night, these words became a prayer I prayed over my daughter, willing her wounded lungs to open and expand, to let every bit of needed air in so that her body could be made whole. And I felt the words as a prayer over me, that in the absence of control or certainty, I might choose to open and expand my own lungs, to breathe deeply and feel the weight of what it means to be human.

There are myriad forces—internal and external—that compel us toward certainty. They tell us that everything can and should be conquered, tamed, defined, controlled, predicted, planned for. I feel those forces—the ones I choose and the ones thrust upon me—in my body. I feel the anxiety they create, the possibilities they limit.

But I can also feel breath. I can pause and turn my attention to what already and always has been taking place within and around me, this movement that I take part in and that is entirely beyond me. I can open and expand my lungs. I can inhale—noticing the familiarity and ease of the rhythm—and I can exhale—knowing that Breath can be held but ultimately never contained. I can take in the God who is as close as the air in my lungs and as deeply, wonderfully mysterious as the human experience, saying God's name each time I do.

God Is . . .

Man corrupt everything, say Shug. He on your box of grits, in your head, and all over the radio. He try to make you think he everywhere. Soon as you think he everywhere, you think he God. But he ain't. Whenever you trying to pray, and man plop himself on the other end of it, tell him to git lost, say Shug. Conjure up flowers, wind, water, a big rock.

—Alice Walker, *The Color Purple*

Earth is so thick with divine possibility that it is a wonder we can walk anywhere without cracking our shins on altars.

—Barbara Brown Taylor, *An Altar in the World*

I love inspiring Internet videos as much as anyone because, well, I'm a human with a beating heart, and because I've yet to hit my quota of seeing unlikely animal friendships or reminders about the goodness of humanity. I'm here for all of it.

But without question, the videos that get me the most are those in which someone who is colorblind is gifted specialized glasses that enable them to see color (incidentally, someone always seems to be cutting onions nearby when I watch them, which is a weird coincidence). A friend or child or spouse surprises their loved one with the glasses, and usually the person has no idea what to expect. They open the box curiously, wondering why they're being filmed, feeling a bit hesitant about what's happening.

The uncertainty continues when finally they open the box to see a pair of sunglasses. "Put them on!" the family cheers. And when they do, it's like time stands still. Suddenly, in an instant, their world changes. They are able to see colors they've never seen before, hues and tones they never could have imagined. They'll twist their head around at every angle, wanting to take it all in as fast as possible yet not wanting to miss a single thing. And almost every single time, they begin to weep. Big muscled men, small children, elderly ladies—they all weep. They've been given access to something that previously was outside of their realm, and their world is busted wide open in full and vibrant color. I can't get enough of these videos. They move me at a guttural level, and they speak a better sermon than any I've yet to write.

What these videos capture is not the world itself changing, the world becoming different, because the colors already existed well before the special lenses were made or put on. It's that the person's world changes. In its current state, their vision grants them access only to certain colors and hues. That's all they have. And then, suddenly, they see. They see beyond, they see more fully, they see more. It was there around them all the time. The trees have always been green. The sky is unfailingly blue. The balloon is red and the playground is purple and everything is what it is. But if you can't see it, you'd never know it. The glasses open up a window into a new world that Always Already Was.

I'm also a sucker for stories about people who've died and come back to life, who've tasted a hint of whatever comes next long enough to be able to speak about it. And one of the most common descriptions these folks share is that they saw colors that don't exist in this realm, colors they can't begin to describe or name because the language for them doesn't exist either. They are overwhelmed by the beauty they glimpsed and are unable to describe it fully.

My journey with an ever-expanding God has been rooted in this conviction, which years ago came to me like an unexpected gift and only continues to become clearer to me: the Divine cannot be described in one color, one tone, one hue; cannot be contained in one image, one metaphor, one symbol; cannot be bound by one tradition, one story, one idea. God is bigger and wider and more than any of our best and worst attempts to name God.

And yet, entire schools of theology and political empires and religious institutions and national identities have been forged through a by and large singular view of God that props up one group of humans and marginalizes others, that allows one set of voices to speak and silences others, that permits one way of thinking and speaking about God and denigrates all others. Sometimes, this happens somewhat unknowingly, perpetuated by folks who should but don't know better. Too many times, the method and intent are clear and calculated.

You can't defend chattel slavery or Jim Crow segregation if God is a Black woman. You can't keep women subordinated in their place if God is Sacred Feminine. You can't deny the dignity and humanity of LGBTQ folks if God dances in and through and around every binary a culture can erect and sacralize. You can't amass weapons and fortresses and call it holy if God is a Vulnerable Peacemaker who transmutes violence rather than perpetuates it.

For too long, much of the world has been colonized by a White male god who is sometimes loving and gracious, who is often violent and greedy and domineering, who is always small. This god colonized my own mind and body, forever keeping me close enough because of my skin color and at a distance because of my sex. I have benefited from this god, shared in his privileges, and I have been wounded by him.

For far too long, a singular image of God has reigned supreme, to the detriment of everyone and everything—even those who look most like this image of God. To critique the singularity of this image and the way it's been weaponized in favor of a few and to the trauma of many is not to dehumanize ones who have dehumanized, to shift a pendulum so that oppressors become oppressed.

Rather, it is to destroy every barrier that keeps humans from seeing themselves fully in God and in one another. It is to speak of a better world where the Divine image reflects the very creation God made, a world that assumes utter abundance and evidences staggering diversity. It is to issue an invitation for every human being to name God in all the colors and words and concepts and sensations and images and bodies and stories available to us.

There's a story in the Hebrew Scriptures about a girl named Hagar, an enslaved young Egyptian owned by Sarah, the matriarch of the Jewish and Christian faiths (see Gen. 16). In the ancient Near Eastern world (and arguably still in many places today), a woman's singular token of status and survival was bearing children. Her value to the community was equal to the proper functioning of her reproductive organs (because, of course, any issue with conception was presumed hers and not that of her male partner). To be unmarried or widowed or barren was to be vulnerable, stigmatized.

It was in this world that Sarah, unable to conceive children, devised a plan. God had promised that she and Abraham would be the forebears of a nation, their descendants more numerous than the stars. The promise seemed laughable, almost cruel. The sky is populated with an infinite number of stars, but Sarah was unsuccessful at populating anything.

So she resorted to what was at the time a common practice: she told her husband Abraham to sleep with Hagar, her slave, so that through her Sarah could bear a child (if you're getting a *Handmaid's Tale* vibe, you're not alone). The literal rending is that she wanted to be "built up" through Hagar. Abraham rapes Hagar—because that is the only appropriate term for sex between two humans with such power differentials where one partner has no power to say no—and she gets pregnant.

The text says that from this point, Hagar began to look "with contempt at her mistress." Many have suggested that Hagar began to feel powerful, that for the first time she had access to some measure of status, and she saw herself—and Sarah—in a new light. Maybe that's true. Humans do all sorts of things in response to trauma. But I wonder if the contempt she felt for Sarah was not at least in part for the ways Hagar had no voice, no power, no agency, for how she was forced to obey Sarah's will and be raped by an old man.

Maybe she viewed the pregnancy with contempt, feeling sudden access to status but all still without her consent. I don't know. What we do know is that, as the story tells us, Sarah began to treat Hagar *brutally*. The text uses the same word that will soon describe the Israelites' torture and oppression at the hands of the Egyptians. So the young girl, pregnant and alone, flees into the desert knowing she likely won't survive in the wilderness but certainly won't survive life at home.

She heads toward Shur, a location on the southern route to Egypt with the same name as one of the Hebrew verbs meaning "to see." She stops at a spring, which in Hebrew is the same word as "eye" (it's almost as if the author is trying to tell us something here). And here at the spring, she encounters God.

We're not told that Hagar cried out to God or summoned God. Perhaps she had heard Abraham and Sarah speak of their deity in peculiar ways even as she prayed to her own Egyptian deities. Regardless, we're told that God saw her in her plight. God asks her where she's coming from and where she's heading, and all she can say is that she is on the run from her mistress, having fled Sarah's brutality.

And in the middle of the desert with its own brutalities, God says that Hagar's son will survive and her descendants will be many. God makes her promises similar to ones given to Abraham and Sarah, the text's central characters. Like Moses in a later chapter, Abraham receives God's name and is told who God is, but here, *Hagar names God*.

A young, enslaved Egyptian girl, the victim of rape, pregnant and alone in the middle of the desert, is the first person in the Bible to name God.

"You are El Roi," she says, "The God who Sees." At a spring named *Beer-lahai-roi*—"Well of the Living One Who Has Seen Me"—

Hagar is seen by God, has an encounter with God, and names God (Gen. 16:13).

It seems to me that the ability to name God requires two things: a willingness to pay attention, and a boldness to speak of what you notice. We're told that God saw and heard Hagar, but she also had to be aware, had to be willing to allow for the absurd possibility that the Divine could visit her in the middle of nowhere. She had to pay attention.

What she saw and heard and felt and experienced, she put into language. She commemorated. She named. She could have dismissed it all as first trimester paranoia, or believed that her lowly status denied her the right to craft Divine titles. But no. That girl put the name of God on her lips and breathed it out like fire.

Part of my work in sitting with individuals in spiritual direction is to listen for the ways they name God. They'll use the word "God" over and over, but when I listen closely, I hear them describe That Stirring Within for More or a Peace That Guides or a sense of Overwhelming Love, and I hear them naming the Divine and breathing out all sorts of ways of getting at what we could even mean when we say "God." I see them unknowingly lift their fingers into the air, pointing at the vast, expanding universe and describing its light and beauty and mystery from various angles. So I help them see their finger pointing in the air, inviting them to keep naming God as they've always done.

I work to help them pay attention—to their bodies, their hearts, their spirits, their thoughts, their emotions, their imaginations—and in the Really Real of their lives to name God. I want them to notice when the Divine is revealed within and around and through them and to know that their sense of this can be articulated, can be symbolized, can be turned into watercolors, can be wrapped in language.

I want it for them, but truthfully, I want it for me too. I'll continue to name God from my embodied reality as a human being, and these will be beautiful and expansive contributions. But I know there is more of God than I can access, there is more light emanating from the moon and stars and galaxies than I can see, and I need other hands willing to reach toward the sky, pointing at these expanding mysteries and putting words to what they notice. And I want to stand closely enough to overhear them.

The world needs humans who aren't interested in colonizing the moon and planting their flag to claim it. The world needs humans open to the entire universe with all of its mysteries and who don't let that stop them from saying something about it.

One of my spiritual practices is to collect names for God. They show up in my experiences and in my prayers, in what I read and what I see, so I take time to notice them. I'm trying to cultivate the discipline of paying attention, to be as bold as an enslaved girl in the ancient Near East who would notice how God shows up and put language to it. Here are some names from my collection:

The Ultimate Ancestor
All That Is
That Which Is beyond Knowing but Not beyond Loving
She Who Is
Ground of All Being
Holy Mystery
She Who Dwells Within
Guiding Light
The Great Allower
Magnificent Other
Relentless Affection
Great Mystery
Infinite Source
The Relationship
The Great Lover
Totally Other, Totally Ours
Eternal Fullness
Ultimate Participant
Most Moved Mover

God Is ...

The Big Tradition
Divine Dance
Inner Knower and Reminder
Absolute Vulnerability between Three
Absolute Love
Great Empowerer
Accompanying Presence
All-Vulnerable
God of the Gallows
Real Presence
Divine Companion
Tender Mother
Prodding One
The More
Ultimate Reality
The Beyond in Our Midst
Loving Presence
The One before Whom All Words Recoil
The Really Real
The Luminous Web That Holds All Things Together
Infinite Compassion
Community of Love
Chief Ancestor
All Loving
The Great Lap
Being Itself
That Than Which Nothing Greater Can Be Conceived
Pure Presence
Power Greater Than Myself
Sacred Spirit
Infinite Compassion
The Great Creator
Living Power
The Force That through the Green Fuse Drives the Flower

Chapter 15

An Energy Flow That Likes to Extend Itself
Infinite Being
Unlimited Supply
The Great Artist
The Light Within
Fundamental Energy
Life Giver
Infinite Flow of Love
An Irresistible Power Not Ourselves
Wisdom Source
Fearless Divine
Oneness
Great Indwelling
Without Fear
Timeless Form
Wholeness
Great Spirit
Relentless Grace
Living Truth
Ineffable One
Energy of Love
Great Forgiver
Holiness Itself
Unconditional Love
The Always Present
Suffering One
Transcendent Mystery
Healing Power
The One Whose Center Is Everywhere and Whose Circumference
    Is Nowhere
Higher Power
Reconciling Force
Transcendent Presence
The Unknown

God Is...

Creative Flow

Source of All Truth

That Which We Cannot Speak of and the One About Whom and
to Whom We Must Never Stop Talking

With Us

The One in and beyond Everything

Liberating Freedom

Always Already Awareness

The Space between Everything

The Welcoming Within

Eternal Now

Living One

Vulnerable Peacemaker

The One Who Sees

Mysteriously Plenty

Voice Calling Me to Live Fully

She Who Restores Our Soul

The Divine Presence in Everyone and Everything

An Infinite Horizon That Pulls Us from within and Pulls us Forward Too

The Light Inside of Everything

A Flow of Energy Willingly Allowed and Willingly Exchanged Without
Requiring Payment In Return

Inner Whole-Making Instinct

The Power Who Exists in All Beings

Mother of Us All

Infinite Primal Source

She Who Steadies Our Inner and Outer Worlds

The Knowable Unknowable

The Absolute

Love

This list is neither exhaustive nor complete and never will be. I'm
just one finger pointing at the universe I inhabit, with my own partic-
ularities and limitedness and faults. But I'll keep pointing up, trying

to describe what I see. And I'll keep looking for others with their hands stretched to the heavens—hands as dark as the night sky and hands brown like clay and tender hands still growing and hands with weathered skin and knotted knuckles. I'll keep listening for voices as diverse as the God who made humanity in her image, as together in our own languages we seek to name the God Who Is.

Epilogue

I know that it feels a kind o' hissin and ticklin' like to see a colored woman get up and tell you about things, and Woman's Rights. We have all been thrown down so low that nobody thought we'd ever get up again; but we have been long enough trodden now; we will come up again, and now I am here.

—Sojourner Truth

You do not need to know precisely what is happening, or exactly where it is all going. What you need is to recognize the possibilities and challenges offered by the present moment, and to embrace them with courage, faith, and hope.

—Thomas Merton

I want to tell you a story about acorns because sometimes—*many times*—a simple story or parable or poem says more than tens of thousands of words could ever hope to, which means perhaps we should have started here.[1]

Once upon a time, in a not-so-far-away land, there was a kingdom of acorns, nestled at the foot of a grand old oak tree. Since the citizens of this kingdom were modern, fully Westernized acorns, they went about their business with purposeful energy; and since they were midlife, baby-boomer acorns, they engaged in a lot of self-help courses. There were seminars called "Getting All You Can out of Your Shell." There were woundedness and recovery groups for acorns who had been bruised in their original fall from the tree. There were spas for oiling and polishing those shells and various acornopathic therapies to enhance longevity and well-being.

One day in the midst of this kingdom there suddenly appeared a knotty little stranger, apparently dropped "out of the blue" by a passing bird. He was capless and dirty, making an immediate negative impression on his fellow acorns. And crouched beneath the oak tree, he stammered out a wild tale. Pointing upward at the tree, he said, "We . . . are . . . that!"

Delusional thinking, obviously, the other acorns concluded, but one of them continued to engage him in conversation: "So tell us, how would we become that tree?"

"Well," he said, pointing downward, "it has something to do with going into the ground . . . and cracking open the shell."

"Insane," they responded. "Totally morbid! Why, then we wouldn't be acorns anymore."

I tell this story often when I teach. It tells the truth slant like Emily Dickinson suggested, a through-the-back-door, delightful surprise encounter. I tell it because I love this little tale, but also because I hate it. Like the acorns repulsed by the stranger's pronouncement, I'm not eager to hear about cracking open and going deep, or about the kind of death that new life requires. It is painful. It is costly. It requires tremendous energy and years of therapy, an appetite for risk and a tolerance for ambiguity. It demands a release from control, an openness to whatever comes, a willingness to be vulnerable. And staying inside my safe shell sounds like a hell of a lot better deal.

But then I realize that I can't stop staring at the oak tree, wondering if the strange acorn is right and imagining what it could mean if he is. And I begin to think that maybe, the pain of going deep below the surface might be worth getting to glimpse what's possible.

Once when I was sitting at the precipice of a new season, I met with my spiritual director. I sensed that I needed to move on, to close a door, to enter into the new. But for as much as I could articulate the reasons why I needed to leave my current context, I could far better name all the risks of doing so. On paper, it was a horrible decision. It made no sense. It was risky at *best*. So I droned on and on about my fears and anxieties and how averse to risk I generally feel.

And then, after listening to me ramble, he quietly asked me a question that changed everything: "What are the risks of staying?" And in an instant, I knew. I realized that I was taking risks regardless, and that it was up to me to decide which ones were worth taking, which risks would move me into a space of flourishing.

There are risks to everything I've proposed here. It's hard to bring into question what you've known of yourself, to interrogate reality and wonder about why you ended up playing small. It's hard to bring into question your sense of God, to consider that perhaps the ways you've come to image God have been just as small. I've felt both fears. I still do.

But every time I come back to the oak tree and imagine the More—more of God, more of myself, more of everything—I realize that this path leads to liberation. I realize that both the shell I've stayed within and the shell placed around the wild Divine are pieced together with fear and shame, and I want to live like an oak tree with roots that sink into materials much more vibrant and lifegiving than those. I want this liberation. I want it for my neighbors, for creation itself.

So I'll sense into the Expanding Impulses that surge within, the very same energy moving the universe into wider and vaster terrain. I'll notice the Divine animating this whole thing and I'll try to put language around it.

When you do the same, will you tell me what you see?

Reflections

In the summers when I was little, my dad and I would spend an afternoon at the AAA office down the road. There, with a yellow highlighter and a giant map, an agent would make a TripTik—a customized road trip planner that helped us navigate whatever part of the country we were about to explore.

I've never been good at reading maps, and I feel immensely grateful for a GPS that just tells me what direction I'm going. But I know that the challenges of any new exploration can be eased with some guideposts.

I offer here practices and reflections to help you further engage with *God Is*. These prompts can reveal access points, places where you can step onto the trail and begin your journey. Whether you explore them alone or in a group, may they offer support for the venture.

- Notice what came up for you as you read each chapter. Where did you feel resistance? Where did you feel deep resonance? What questions surfaced for you?
- Reflect back on your own expanding sense of self and God. Chart out on paper the various seasons of your life. Give them a name, a color, an image. For each, make note of what your primary image of God was at the time. How have these evolved? How have *you* evolved?
- As you reflect on the images of God that you've held in past and current seasons, consider if there are any that no longer square with

your sense of self and of the Divine. Are there any images that are too small and are keeping you small? Make a list, and thoughtfully name the ways they may have served you or helped you (if at all). Then prayerfully release them, affirming God's invitation for you to expand along with your sense of God.

- Identify the metaphor that you felt most resistance to. Hold curiosity around what might be behind the resistance. Notice the emotions connected with the resistance (anger, fear, shame, etc.). Do you still need to resist in order to survive your given season? Has this resisting helped you in some way? Or do you sense a stirring within to begin engaging this metaphor? Remember, there is no wrong or right here. There may be an image that you *never* feel comfortable engaging. Be patient with yourself. Be led by curiosity and not self-judgment.

- Seat yourself in front of a large mirror. If it feels safe and comfortable to do so, consider doing this naked. Scan yourself—your body, your heart, your mind, your talents, your spirit—and note ways that you particularly and beautifully reflect the Divine. Celebrate these and return to them often.

- Consider what metaphors you would add to this collection. Write up a description of how you've experienced a particular image of God and, if it feels safe, share it with someone. Ask them to share with you the images of God that they hold close.

- Seat yourself in a comfortable, safe place. Take time to breathe deeply and slowly. Ground yourself. Scan your body and notice what it feels like. When you feel ready, begin imagining God in a particular form. It can be one of the metaphors explored here or a different one entirely. Notice what God looks like, feels like, sounds like, seems like. As best as you're able, allow your imagination to take over. Engage the God you imagine. Ask questions, and notice what you hear or sense in return. Suspend judgment and critique here. You are in a realm of uncertainty and wonder and play, so allow for that sense of freedom and playfulness. You are not seeking to master anything here, simply to have an experience. As you conclude the exercise, ask Wisdom Within if there's any invitation being extended to you here.

- In the evening, reflect on your dominant thoughts and beliefs throughout the day. For each, ask yourself what the image of God is behind them. Is it one that you believe in? Does it reveal a distorted image that you need to reconsider? If so, take a moment to bring to mind a particular image of God that is generous, loving, and kind. What might that God say to the thoughts and beliefs you named?
- Begin your own collection of names for God. Start a list in your journal or on your phone. Whenever you read or hear or experience something that feels like it names the Divine, make note.

Notes

Chapter 1

1. If you *haven't*: stop reading this, watch all four seasons—twice—then come back.

Chapter 2

1. Augustine, *Sermon* 67. Augustine's sermon may be found at https://www.newadvent.org/fathers/160367.htm.

Chapter 3

1. Spiritual direction is an ancient practice of companioning another person as they seek to discern and explore the Divine in their lives and in the world.

2. Elizabeth A. Johnson, *She Who Is: The Mystery of God in Feminist Theological Discourse* (New York: Herder & Herder, 1992), 4.

3. Origen, *Fragments on 1 Corinthians.*

4. Clement of Alexandria, *Pedagogues* II.33.2.

5. Tertullian, *On the Apparel of Women* 1.1.

6. Tertullian, *On the Dress of Women*, in *Patrologia Graeca*, 70.59.

7. Chrysostom, *Homily on Genesis 2.*

8. Chrysostom, *Homily 9 on First Timothy.*

9. Chrysostom, *The Kind of Women Who Ought to Be Taken as Wives.*

10. Augustine, *On Genesis Literally Interpreted* 9.5.9.

11. Augustine, *On Genesis Literally Interpreted* 11.42.

12. Augustine, *The Trinity* 12.7.10.

13. Augustine, *Letter to Laetus* 243.10.

14. Saint Albert the Great, *Questions concerning on Animals* XV.11.

15. Thomas Aquinas, *Summa Theologica* I. 92 Article 1, Reply to Objection 1.

16. Martin Luther, *Commentary on Genesis*, Chapter 2, Part V, 27b.

17. Martin Luther, *Luther's Works*, ed. Hilton C. Oswald, vol. 28, *Commentaries on 1 Corinthians 7, 1 Corinthians 15, Lectures on 1 Timothy* (St. Louis: Concordia, 1973), 12.94.

18. John Calvin, "Commentary on John 20," "Calvin's Commentary on the Bible," https://www.studylight.org/commentaries/eng/cal/john-20.html, 1840–57.

19. John Calvin, *Commentary on Corinthians* (Grand Rapids: Christian Classics Ethereal Library), 1:299, https://www.ccel.org/ccel/c/calvin/cal com39/cache/calcom39.pdf.

20. John Calvin, *John Calvin's Bible Commentaries on St. Paul's Epistles to Timothy, Titus, and Philemon* (Altenmünster, Germany: Jazzybee Verlag Jürgen Beck), 49.

21. John Knox, *The First Blast of the Trumpet against the Monstrous Regiment of Women* (Westminster: Archibald Constable & Co., 1895), v.

22. Knox, *First Blast of the Trumpet*, 20.

23. The acronym BIPOC stands for "Black, Indigenous, and People of Color."

24. Johnson, *She Who Is*, 15.

Chapter 4

1. "What Does 'Born in the U.S.A.' Really Mean?," *NPR*, March 26, 2019, https://www.npr.org/2019/03/26/706566556/bruce-springsteen -born-in-the-usa-american-anthem.

2. "What Does 'Born in the U.S.A.' Really Mean?"

3. Barbara Brown Taylor, "The Parable of the Fearful Investor," Duke

University Chapel, November 13, 2011, YouTube video, https://www.you
tube.com/watch?v=sEzT7hFdhLU.

4. Taylor, "Parable of the Fearful Investor."

5. Taylor, "Parable of the Fearful Investor."

Chapter 5

1. Incidentally, this song played at the last silent disco I attended, and if
you ever happen to hear the explicit version that close to your ear canals,
brace yourself.

2. It is essential to note that this has never applied equally to all men.
Certainly, one's class, race, and sexual orientation inform the ways one can
still be othered through God language even if their biological sex is male.
What qualifies as "masculine" is entirely socially constructed.

3. Christena Cleveland, *She Who Cannot Be Shamed, Tamed, or Contained*. Digital PDF.

4. Elizabeth A. Johnson, *She Who Is: The Mystery of God in Feminist
Theological Discourse* (New York: Herder & Herder, 1992), 39.

5. Richard Rohr, *Naked Now* (Chestnut Ridge, NY: Crossroads, 2009),
131.

Chapter 6

1. Karen Baker-Fletcher, *Dancing with God: The Trinity from a Womanist
Perspective* (St. Louis: Chalice Press, 2006), 70.

2. The Mesopotamian creation myth known in Akkadian as Enuma
Elish, the opening words of the myth meaning "when on high."

3. The Epic of Gilgamesh.

Chapter 7

1. For information on Preemptive Love see https://preemptivelove
.org/.

Chapter 8

1. The Hebrew word *ruach*, translated as "spirit," "breath," or "wind," is feminine.

Chapter 9

1. This can be especially true for women of color when—as a result of systemic racism and enduring myths about Black bodies—healthcare providers don't believe their pain or don't provide appropriate care.

2. Valarie Kaur, *See No Stranger: A Memoir and Manifesto of Revolutionary Love* (New York: One World, 2020), xiii.

Chapter 10

1. If I was anything other than a straight, White woman, this moment would have come *much* earlier in my life. Privilege can protect you from some things, but only for so long.

2. I use this modified term here as a way of noting the power of our language. Rather than "kingdom," an imperialistic, militaristic word (which indeed can helpfully demonstrate the political realities of God), "kindom" reflects a new kind of humanity, a beloved community. I'm grateful to Womanist theologians like Wilda Gafney and Emilie Townes for helping expand my vision.

Chapter 11

1. "Bishop Attacks Display of Female Christ Figure," *New York Times*, April 25, 1984, https://www.nytimes.com/1984/04/25/nyregion/bishop-attacks-display-of-female-christ-figure.html.

2. Andrew J. Schmutzer, "Spiritual Formation and Sexual Abuse: Embodiment, Community, and Healing," *Journal of Spiritual Formation & Soul Care* 2, no. 1 (2009): 68. I choose here to focus primarily on women's and girls' experiences because of my particular background and experience,

and because women remain the primary victims of sexual trauma that are by and large perpetrated by men. But as these statistics clearly show, boys and men endure the same traumas—with less frequency, but with no less impact.

3. Schmutzer, "Spiritual Formation," 69.

4. Mindy Makant, "Transforming Trauma: The Power of Touch and the Practice of Anointing," *Word and World* 34:2 (Spring 2014): 161.

5. Brittany J. Arias and Chad V. Johnson, "Voices of Healing and Recovery from Childhood Sexual Abuse," *Journal of Child Sexual Abuse* 22:7 (2013): 823.

6. Nancy Nienhuis, "Theological Reflections on Violence and Abuse," *The Journal of Pastoral Care and Counseling* 59:1–2 (Spring–Summer 2005): 110.

7. Judith Herman, *Trauma and Recovery: The Aftermath of Violence—From Domestic Abuse to Political Terror* (New York: Basic Books, 1997), 12.

8. Herman, *Trauma and Recovery*, 13.

9. Herman, *Trauma and Recovery*, 14.

10. Herman, *Trauma and Recovery*, 14.

11. Herman, *Trauma and Recovery*, 14.

12. Certainly a penal substitutionary atonement theory is behind many of these dangerous theologies, but it is not the only source.

13. Richard Beck, *Reviving Old Scratch: Demons and the Devil for Doubters and the Disenchanted* (Minneapolis: Fortress, 2016), 175.

14. As Kimberlé Crenshaw has so rightly shown us, this kind of action always demands a clear understanding of intersectionality, i.e., the interconnectedness of all systems of power, discrimination, and dehumanization. Theologian Nancy Nienhuis affirms the same:

> When we put intimate violence within the context of power relations that are interrelated and that reinforce each other, then we understand that the problem of intimate violence is much bigger than just getting some guy to stop hitting some woman. And we further understand that other oppressive forces, like racism and class bias, are all part of an epistemology that values human beings

differently depending on how closely they resemble those in society with the most power and privilege. We cannot begin to dismantle one system of oppression and the violence it causes unless we are willing to take on all of them. (Nancy Nienhuis, "Theological Reflections," 121)

Chapter 12

1. This ease of associating anything "dark" with evil has its roots in White supremacy, as so much does.

2. My friend Richard Beck offers a helpful approach on this front. Check out *Reviving Old Scratch: Demons and the Devil for Doubters and the Disenchanted* (Minneapolis: Fortress, 2016).

3. Developed by Richard Schwartz, Internal Family Systems is a powerful therapeutic approach that utilizes Family Systems theory to name and integrate these parts of ourselves.

Chapter 14

1. Aldous Huxley, *Brave New World* (New York: HarperCollins, 1932), 240.

2. Richard Rohr, *Naked Now* (New York: Crossroad, 2009), 24.

Epilogue

1. The version I share here is from Beatrice Chestnut, *The Complete Enneagram* (Berkeley, CA: She Writes Press, 2013), 38–39. Chestnut takes this from Cynthia Bourgeault's *The Wisdom Way of Knowing* (San Francisco: Jossey-Bass, 2003), 64–65. Bourgeault cites Scottish neurologist Maurice Nicoll as the story's original teller.

Selected Bibliography

This list includes a few of the texts that have companioned me in recent years, leaving an imprint on me and on this book.

Baker-Fletcher, Karen. *Dancing with God: The Trinity from a Womanist Perspective*. St. Louis: Chalice Press, 2006.

Bell, Rob. *What We Talk about When We Talk about God*. New York: HarperOne, 2014.

Cameron, Julia. *The Artist's Way: A Spiritual Path to Higher Creativity*. New York: Tarcher Perigree, 2016.

Gaskin, Ina May. *Guide to Childbirth*. New York: Bantam Books, 2003.

Guenther, Margaret. *Holy Listening: The Art of Spiritual Direction*. Cambridge, MA: Cowley Publications, 1992.

Herman, Judith. *Trauma and Recovery: The Aftermath of Violence—From Domestic Abuse to Political Terror*. New York: Basic Books, 1997.

Johnson, Elizabeth A. *She Who Is: The Mystery of God in Feminist Theological Discourse*. New York: Herder & Herder, 1992.

Kaur, Valarie. *See No Stranger: A Memoir and Manifesto of Revolutionary Love*. New York: One World, 2020.

Kendi, Ibram X. *Stamped from the Beginning: The Definitive History of Racist Ideas in America*. New York: Bold Type Books, 2017.

Lipsky, Laura Van Dermoot. *Trauma Stewardship: An Everyday Guide to Caring for Self While Caring for Others*. Oakland: Berrett-Koehler, 2009.

Selected Bibliography

Oliver, Mary. *Devotions: The Selected Poems of Mary Oliver.* New York: Penguin Press, 2017.

Rohr, Richard. *Naked Now.* New York: Crossroad, 2009.

Soughers, Tara K. *Beyond a Binary God: A Theology for Trans* Allies.* New York: Church Publishing, 2018.

Taylor, Barbara Brown. *An Altar in the World: A Geography of Faith.* New York: HarperOne, 2009.

Taylor, Sonya Renee. *The Body Is Not an Apology: The Power of Radical Self-Love.* Oakland: Berrett-Koehler, 2021.

Tsabary, Shefali. *The Conscious Parent: Transforming Ourselves, Empowering Our Children.* Vancouver: Namaste Publishing, 2010.

Van der Kolk, Bessel. *The Body Keeps the Score: Brain, Mind, and Body in the Healing of Trauma.* New York: Penguin Publishing Group, 2015.

Walker, Alice. *The Color Purple.* New York: Penguin Books, 2019.